Endorsements

"I felt Christine's pain, sadness, courage, and strength when reading her book. She captured her story in a meaningful and educational manner. I have learned so much information from reading her book."
—Ela Orlowska, LPC, NCC, MS

"The book is a moving and personal account of the pain of divorce and shares the best ways to heal and re-engage in who *you* are, through God's mercy and His plan for you."
—Kim Dickie

"Having personal experience with her traumatizing divorce, Christine gives therapeutic useful help and information in a compassionate and caring manner. I was so thankful to be one of the first people to read Christine's book while going through my divorce. Her book provided me with some solace and emotional relief. Knowing that she had experienced the same difficulties and came out the other side stronger, happier, and free, gave me hope that I could too."
—Jennifer Cox MS, SW

"This book is an inspiration for any woman who is going through a divorce. An excellent read for any woman who is experiencing the breakup of her family."
—Carolyn Fisher

A Heart's Betrayal

A Heart's Betrayal

Tools for Christian Women Recovering from Divorce

Christine Cantilena Barnes

Copyright © 2024 by Christine Cantilena Barnes

All rights reserved. No part of this book may be reproduced or transmitted in any form or by any means, electronic or mechanical, including photocopying, recording, or any information storage and retrieval system, without permission in writing from the author.

ISBN: 978-1-6653-0806-9 - Paperback
eISBN: 978-1-6653-0807-6 - eBook

These ISBNs are the property of BookLogix for the express purpose of sales and distribution of this title. The content of this book is the property of the copyright holder only. BookLogix does not hold any ownership of the content of this book and is not liable in any way for the materials contained within. The views and opinions expressed in this book are the property of the Author/Copyright holder, and do not necessarily reflect those of BookLogix.

Library of Congress Control Number: 2023923265

☉This paper meets the requirements of ANSI/NISO Z39.48-1992 (Permanence of Paper)

0 4 1 8 2 4

Changinghopecounseling.com

To all those who have suffered great loss in their lives due to the aftermath of divorce, including children. You are now a survivor or on your way to the other side. Your life has a great purpose. I know this to be true because your journey is not over yet.

I'd like to share something that stuck with me for a long time after watching a popular television show called, Suits: "You know how I judge a man's character, not by how he treats his equals, but by how he treats his underlings."

Contents

Acknowledgments   *ix*
Preface   *xi*
Introduction   *xiii*

Chapter 1	Who Are You and Who Do You Want to Be?	1
Chapter 2	Who Teaches Us Commitment and What Does It Really Mean to Us?	23
Chapter 3	What Is Domestication and Is It Real in Marriage?	45
Chapter 4	How Real Is Narcissism and Gaslighting?	57
Chapter 5	A Life Can Be Made Shameless	67
Chapter 6	Society and It's Darkness	79
Chapter 7	The Many Broken Pieces of Our Children	95
Chapter 8	Why Do Men Stray?	113
Chapter 9	When to Let Go Before You Are Lost	119
Chapter 10	Damage Control and Proactive Behavior	131
Chapter 11	Is Healing Really Possible?	147
Chapter 12	Educating Our Legal Team and What Effects It Will Have on Us	159
Chapter 13	The Aftermath of Divorce	185
Chapter 14	What Is Your Part?	197
Chapter 15	Divorce and Client Testimonies	209

Epilogue   223
Afterword   225
Notes   227

Acknowledgments

To my amazing friends and family who were such supportive and large parts of the completion of this book. Each chapter has great meaning to me and reveals various seasons in my life, both happy and sad. As I am looking down from the hill of victory, I can see how life's significant pain has led to the growth inside me, which has made me the strongest version of myself. My guardian angel never left my side nor did the sturdiness of God the Almighty.

I hope my experiences will lead you in the direction of attaining the authentic meaning of true love and healthier relationships. Here's to the boy who thought I hung the moon and gave me great purpose! My sweet son Romeo, I have loved you for so many years. I cherish you more than you will ever realize with so many powerful memories we have made together. Your brightness shines in my heart always. May you have eternal integrity, honor, and character always, especially in the presence of a woman, particularly your future wife, and behind closed doors. For people to continue to say and believe, "Your son has the heart of a godly servant," this meant so much to me hearing it from so many when you were a young boy in church on Wednesday evenings at the dinners.

I could not end the dedication without a special acknowledgement to Linda, Ela, Kelli, Selena, Christina, Susie, Milton, Lynda, and Jennifer: such devoted friends during college and work, and now so many years after. They know my truth first-hand and have been my rock through this enduring process. Their constant belief in me has made me trust in things getting better when nothing made sense. Writing this book was an abiding journey that I saw to the end. This is one of my greatest accomplishments which I will never forget.

Always know where your *true north lies*. Betrayal is the ultimate sacrifice of one person for a heart's desire at any cost, even one's wedding vows. Understanding your true north, value, and moral system can help a person fight against the most relentless tidal wave of grief, shame, and recovery.

Preface

You may be asking yourself why your marriage journey has taken this unexpected turn in life or how you will be strong enough to rebuild your life during or after the process of divorce. I was looking for a way to soften the shock of the last years of my marriage, so I wrote this book in hopes to help others who have suffered immense grief.

I lived in a fictitious marriage not in the beginning, however, by year six and the many years after, I totally lost myself in the process, and I began to realize it was time to get back to who I am and what I stood for during this life-changing event of divorce.

The following pages come from a heartfelt sense of knowledge of the Bible and what marriage is built on. You can be rock-solid following God's word or instead, a fraud with a hollow marital commitment that is only is good as the paper it is written on. If you are the victim of later, you may want to continue reading. What most people desire to know while grieving divorce and the loss of their husband, wife, and family is how to move forward and still have purpose. On even a more complex level, you may encounter the feelings of intense loss and anger, coupled with aloneness, when trying to regain your personal sense of self and, moreover, your placement in the community again.

The better version of you can all be achieved with great effort and continued belief in yourself and who you were created to be. One of the most important endeavors you are to face is knowing who you are now and who you will become after such a personal tragedy. Unwarranted divorce is somewhat of a test or challenge to find your faith, level of forgiveness, inner courage and self-esteem once more. It is like being in a deep well and sinking to the very bottom until one day you realize that you are better than that.

Many confusing thoughts will arise out of the ashes of your dissolved marriage. Will everyone still embrace you the same after your divorce? How does divorce change our inner souls and outlooks on life? What will it feel like to not be married any longer? Will non-divorced people ever understand the depths of defeat and damage that many divorces leave behind, and still have empathy for you? The answers are all in the pages to follow.

Introduction

My downward journey of divorce began one hot summer day when my young son and I were riding in the car with my former husband. We were catching a plane to Florida for a summer vacation. I knew for many months that our status quo in marriage was off kilter (less time together, more work involvement, and more distance intimately). I chose not to look at the status of our marriage for fear of knowing my great intuitions and suspicions could be true. I will tell you to be faithfully discerning and listen to your intuition and your gut. It is generally right.

My story all began with an odd thirty-minute phone call in the car on the way to the airport during the start of our vacation. My former husband and I had our phones programed to come on to the car speaker. This time, and many others before this, my husband's phone did not audibly link up to the speaker in our new Range Rover.

Instead, I heard muffled words coming from the phone, but the volume of the phone became harder and harder to hear as the volume button was casually lowered. At that moment, I felt erased as if I was not sitting in the car and had no authority or leverage in our marriage. My life felt like I had just stepped into an endless puddle of sorrow with no chance of escaping. I was hopelessly wondering why this was happening right in front of me as if I was not there. I began that day accepting the truth of a failed and secretive side of my marriage.

The tone of the conversation I heard from my former husband's side of the conversation did not seem right for a business call, and I clearly felt a strong negative power residing over my surroundings. I sensed a type of silent strangulation in the car, with nowhere to go, and tried to be calm, breathe deep, and avoid any confrontation because my son was nearby. I could tell by the tone of his voice this was where respect for me was absent. I decided to just keep things simple by ignoring what was unfolding. My child was in the backseat, so we began playing the license tag game to lighten things up. I would have done anything to keep this awful secret from my child.

The duration of the drive, I wondered what type of person calls a married man with his wife and child just inches away during a family vacation. How has that type of boldness, stealing family time become so cavalier and accepted? My former husband had a normal job, and the magnitude of his work was never a life-or-death situation. I noticed the phone calls became more frequent from the same number and more secretive leading up to the trip. Every time I asked about the phone calls there was rarely any regard for explanations. The motto was "work hard, play harder and ask for forgiveness later." I often wonder how that represented evidence of a Christian man's character.

Upon arrival to our rented beach house, I noticed it was not the usual accommodation we had in the past. Not to sound entitled, but we had always stayed in clean and nice places on the beach. This was an old, dingy house several blocks from the beach. As we approached the house, it had overgrown weeds and trash in the front yard. It was dreary and felt like the wrong vacation house or a last-minute choice with little effort put into planning the vacation. It felt like someone else had made the reservation that did not know us or care about the quality of our family vacation.

Prior to this vacation, I had several back and ankle surgeries that prevented me from long walks, especially in the heat and from a place so far from the ocean. At first, I thought it was an oversight booking this house, but my former husband acted as though it was perfect. As we unpacked our things, there was an urgent need for him to leave my son and I at this house alone. The request for suntan lotion seemed an emergency, as my former husband went out late that evening to get it. He stated he was going to the CVS just around the corner, but nothing made sense in his urgency. I prayed these odd events would disappear, but I soon realized this was that God was revealing truth to me after many years of praying for clear certainty. This pseudo vacation was going to be the place to end our twenty-one years of marriage, and it was.

That evening my former husband's shiny red rental convertible Mustang zoomed out of the rental house's drive (this was also a car type that we have never rented before) and did not arrive back for several hours. As I sat in the dark on the cold cement of the garage's steps of the strange Florida home, I began to cry, wondering why things got so out of hand in my marriage. Before I had a chance to ponder that thought, the shiny rental car pulled into the garage, top down, windows down, and there was a familiar female's voice laughing on the car speaker. All of the sudden my stomach dropped, truth was truth, and my former husband's cell phone was connected to the car speakers. Remarkable coincidence. It was the hardest, saddest, and last vacation that I ever encountered with my former husband and child. That night, there were more tears and secrets revealed than I could ever have expected. From 1 a.m. to approximately 8 a.m., we argued about so many things that had been leading up to this awful place of truth.

At first, my former husband told me there was no one else. However, shortly after this statement, he took his phone into the bathroom, locked the door, and began reprogramming and deleting all his messages as I would later learn. I was able to see several of them as we fought over his phone. They were all in code, so it became apparent I was the only one unable to decode it. While I looked over at my son during our argument, just several feet away, he sat alone on the lanai for over six hours that morning. He was not permitted to come inside where we argued. This felt dreadful while I watched him sitting beside the pool looking over at me. Our family's future was dissolving like grains of sand in the bottom of the ocean. He would have an entirely different life, and so would I, when we returned home.

Divorce is one of the most common and easy deceptions of one's life, believing someone you love would even consider divorcing you. My marriage was a festering wound that was never able to heal and crippled me. It seemed like there was no prosthesis yet made for this type of brokenness.

Divorce could possibly be the highest, publicly sought-after legal action for those disappointed with their current marriages. It can be concluded that for some divorced persons, empowerment by great justification for their exit in marriage with no merit and for purely selfish reasons. For the latter, I believe many see leaving is a better option than staying in an honored commitment and learning to work together as promised on each wedding vow. The thought that "the grass is greener on the other side" is such an escapist thought, but many weak-minded people follow it thinking there is somehow more out in the dating world than what they have in their marriage. This makes the idea of resolution for a couple so much more difficult than maybe even forty years ago.

Even for Christians, there is a myriad of selfish reasons why marriages fail. Our faith does appear to protect us as a shield from the evil. Affairs can be one of the top reasons marriages get stuck in dark places and cannot re-stabilize. They used to be thought of as scarlet letters, shameful to admit or even talk about, being such an embarrassment for a couple. Today, it seems the intensity of negativity is diminished and is replaced with acceptance, as an affair has become a less disreputable topic, now suitable for a lunch conversation. How can society be so desensitized toward the remorse of those who engage in infidelity? Is this what we want our children to grow up and believe, that divorce is just the way of life?

My opinion on this topic of divorce is that darkness resides among us in this world, but it has become loftier and more addictively inviting as the years pass. Deceit and deception have almost become an accepted way of life in many pockets of our society, while accountability has shrunk like an old t-shirt. I think the loss of God in schools, government, and a push for the "me too generation" has not helped. Lack of humility and a high sense of pride has brought major downfalls in human behavior, causing more marriages to soar south. I was forced to accept the most-used legal untruths of "irreconcilable differences" as the reason for my divorce. I wonder if it is just another name used to cover up the selfish lack of discipline, honor, obedience, forgiveness, and connection to a high level of pride in couples today.

Firsthand, I was brought to my knees in this dreadful situation called divorce in 2017. It affected my soul and my physical well-being. As my divorce process itself, it felt like a steel axe breaking me into million invisible bits. I discovered that broken heartedness and poor health are intertwined with threatening divorces. There were many times when I had to pick up the pieces of myself that had fallen apart, like pieces of a mirror with sharp cutting edges. At times, my life felt almost unrecognizable. Additionally, I remember times of even holding a washcloth over my mouth to muffle my screams in the bathroom while my son was just feet away in his room getting ready for school. The sadness and unfolding truth were insurmountable.

The departure of the person I trusted with my heart, life, family, child, and future, plunged me into hopelessness. The tenderness of love and desire to believe in loyalty, commitment, and hope for a Godly reconciliation, now seemed impossible for my marriage.

Few people that I have met in a lifetime can say they have true integrity and honorable transparency in their marriages. However, I do know some awesome couples, just not a multitude. I cannot understand why it is rare to find spouses like these today, even though I know they exist. We all sin and make mistakes, and perfection can't be attained in this world but only in heaven. If you are busy hiding secrets, then you leave the door open to become even more unscrupulous.

Forgiveness can be a positive choice. As long as both players are willing to show their cards. Lose your pride and pray for the Holy Spirit to enter your heart. So many marriages can be healthy, mended, and made whole again by God if everyone else can just move out of His way. There is hope.

I commend those who tried fighting for their marriages. It is possible with great forgiveness and an open heart for redemption to occur even when we have nothing left. Rebuilding and resetting are often required. For others, the path of divorce is inevitable. Divorce is mentally draining because it wrings our hearts out until there is no blood flow left to pump. The body seems to be put in a shock-like state, almost starving and wilting like an old, dying flower. This is why many have increased medical and emotional declines. This is called frozen fright and means that the body and mind are somewhat paralyzed.

There is an amazing author, Bessel Van Der Kolk M.D., who wrote a book many years ago called *The Body Keeps the Score*. It explains how events can cause you trauma and post-traumatic stress syndrome (PTSD) because your body never forgets it. Physical pain can haunt you until you are ready to do the work of recovery. Divorce put my body through a state of shock physically and mentally. I felt its crushing teeth on my neck. It seemed to go on for endless months and I thought it would never end.

Divorce is so very powerful; it comes like a thief in the night and often forces a spouse to accept circumstances and their valued ideals are no longer possible. As soon as the word "divorce" is physically spoken, the negativity seems to strip away your confidence, self-esteem, loving tenderness, benevolent memories, empathy, and compassion. There is no "good divorce,"; this is ridiculous thinking because it is painful and steals a portion of your innocence, while allowing society to find a sense of complacency toward this way of life. There is nothing worse for me than to hear, "This is your new normal." I am sorry but there is nothing normal about it.

I can still hear those actual words echoed from one pastor I knew for 22 years, who said, "You must just accept this is your new normal." These words tore through my soul — as this is a person I trusted for help and had been so transparent with my destructive marriage. Even though this comment almost turned my faith inside out, it taught me a valuable lesson in life. Even ministers, priests, and holy devoted persons are vulnerable and accepting to the worldly ways. It seems shattering when our spiritual principles that we have loved and believed in with all our hearts turn out to be less than we had hoped.

Anyone can betray us even a person with years of faith. It is responses like these, from clergy, that caused me to move my church home, after so many happy years, shortly after my divorce. I knew that to stay aligned with my values, morals, and ethics, a search for a new beginning needed to start. I went back to a church home that I also had attended while I was married. They have assisted me in another time of crisis. In the earlier years of my marriage, my husband had accepted a job in another state. He had never discussed or even informed me of it. I had to hear from my friend who was also a pet sitter that no one was coming to feed the animals for days. Then, I also heard it later from his family who were so proud of him for accepting a job in another state which I didn't even know existed. I never knew pain like being ousted from a family. Every member acted as though I was crazy to be upset over this incident that would have changed my entire life again. The betrayal was crystal clear at this point.

The church back then, took a bold stance and phoned my husband at the time. They told him it was best to immediately return home and come in for an appointment to discuss him leaving the state and accepting a job in VA without my knowledge of this event in our marriage. After some insightful counseling sessions through the church, we seemed to be back on track again until he left, making yet another major decision without my knowledge to quit his current job and work for another company for what he believed was a better position. This was so incredibly hurtful. I felt like he did not value me or any opinion that I may give. I felt like a prop mirroring a wife and mother. Maybe we looked like the perfect family on the outside, but it was anything but the truth.

I was lucky that I went back to this church after my divorce. I remembered it had a backbone where many churches may not have stood up for me and called "a spade a spade." Familiarity is not always the answer in difficult times, and our last church did not seem like a good fit with all the memories of my former marriage. I know the only person I must answer to in life is God. From that choice, I now lead a Bible study and Bible Brunches in my home and am so blessed by amazing ladies and men that truly put Christ first. This helped me align in one of my most honorable values, commitment.

It was so hard to fathom that I was now divorced. A vicious

divorce process does not just ruin the union of a once-committed couple but can have long-lasting effects on you as an individual. I found myself now as a single parent. Stuck in a merry-go-round, trying to co-parent with an impossible situation. I had to battle for my son in constant custody fights over ridiculous things such as therapy, medical procedures, and school issues. It seemed that I had to almost earn the right and prove that I had cared for and nurtured my son from life support at the hospital until even years when the major decline of the relationship. It made me question all the many years of care and devotion which seemingly went unnoticed. Trying to regain normalcy and respect and continue mothering my son was both made impossible, humiliating, and embarrassing throughout his High School years. It truly came down to who had enough fight and money left to continue the court battles even after the divorce.

In most divorces each parent will need to share the 4 items to manage a child's life through high school graduation. These items are religious care, education, medical care, and extracurricular activities. I knew his medical history better than anyone. I had over 500 saved documents on all his medication, various specialists, surgeries, allergies, and testing. I always believed he was a miracle of God being born and surviving so many serious health endeavors. I knew every doctor of his on a very personal level. I fought for his medical and spiritual health. His father was given education and extracurricular activities. Little did I know that this would be the breaking point of the closeness and tenderness with my son we had shared for so many years. As a mother, you must always be smart about which one of these items you choose to manage. In the end, I assume that you could lose no matter which two areas you received. Some spouses can actively use them to highjack the other parent, make them seem like the bad guy, or to deliberately steal time away from the other parent. They can choose a sport or something that takes an enormous amount of time and energy so when they are back with you, they are constantly tired and uninterested in other things that you may want to share.

As a Christian, or even non-Christian, who you allow to mentor your child in any teachings, especially spiritual, could have hidden agendas that you are not aware of. I was very fortunate that I had a wonderful man to help me son get involved with evening events with other kids his age from church. It truly was a blessing. This intervention worked out for a while until other circumstances began to get in the way when my son was in his father's care. It began to grow more difficult to keep him involved with Christian activities, his mentor, and other kids. It can be a true setback when your child does not have a godly man centered in his life. Make certain that you truly trust the people you put your child around during, and after divorce, to offer proper guidance, instead of poor theology and advice.

Even though divorce can be emotionally strangling, paralyzing almost, some successfully overcome it with great mentors supporting them. Know that *grace smashes* pride and injustices *and* rebuilds entire nations—so reflect on what it can do for marriages in need. Never ever forget Psalm 147:3: "He heals the brokenhearted and bandages their wounds."

Why is it so hard to reconcile? Why do people want to give up instead of wanting to work out their differences in a marriage? This book will help you understand this dilemma through a devouring journey that can suck the life out from any living and loving human. It will highlight when communication has failed at every level and when one or both parties decide to throw in the towel. This book will examine why society has reached a level of inconsistency in their faith as well. I mention this because I was taught as a young girl that when people take their vows seriously, it is until death. I don't remember any clause that says, "Until we find another, a replacement, or want our singleness back."

Some of our society is so entitled and insensitive toward the topic of honoring commitment. It is almost like the last twenty years has desensitized us towards divorce, encouraging us that it is honorable to go against commitment, not to just one another, but to God Himself. Are we no longer God fearing?

Divorce has become second nature to many and seems easy for non-Christians and Christians to quickly sign away their marriages after their "tolerance level" has been met. I do not understand why God allows some marriages to heal and avoid divorce, and allows other marriages inevitably wind up in tragic divorce. However, it is increasingly evident that some of what we face today has little remedy outside of God's intervention. He is still in the business of miracles and can soften hearts like no one else.

I personally believe marriage is for us to grow stronger in our values together with one another; instead, it seems divorce is being brought to the table with lawyers fighting for each team when they do not even know you. Your marriage is thrown in the garbage can with the rest of the trash and becomes just another, every day, transaction. We have grown stronger in irresponsibility and hardening our hearts, but this does not need to be the end. We just need to make a swift U- turn back to our heavenly Father. I leave you with these powerful words from writer Sarah Jeanne Browne[1], who stated in an article, *How to Let Go of Fear, Worry, and Indecision*, from *Forbes* magazine, "A dead end may lead you to a detour. A struggle may lead you to your strength. A loss may lead you to a lesson. A regret may lead you to redemption. An obstacle may lead you to an opportunity."

I know there is so much good to be found in this world;

however, you must look sometimes in unexpected places. When you look at how far you have come, even though the pain, suffering, and unbelief of things you never imagined could happen to you, then you will see there is always still more to achieve in your life, even after your divorce. You will make it now like you've made it before; there is no reason to believe differently.

My story is about finding the strength to grow through pure understanding and recognition of your own shortcomings. By sharing this journey with you, I will give you the tools and resources that I acquired during and after my divorce that can help you heal and become victorious on your journey as well.

I wrote this book primarily for women as a guide to minimize pain and suffering during a divorce while equipping those desiring more knowledge with information about relationships and divorce at their fingertips.

I am a Christian, first and foremost, a caring and emotional human being, a mother, daughter, sister, child of God, and entrepreneur. Even though this book is intended for primarily for female readers going through the struggles of divorce, it is not to dismiss that the same atrocities do happen to men as well. The advice in this book might help them too.

I am training you in the nuts and bolts of surviving divorce like a sports playlist: what to expect, avoid, and handle in the face of divorce and turmoil. I invite you to take a journey with me and learn more about exploring the facets of broken relationships, divorce, our legal system, developing a proper support system (friends, family, and co-workers), finding and renewing yourself, healing, and understanding God's help. I pray for each one of my readers that you will be able to learn from my experiences and avoid pitfalls, as you grow immeasurably in your journey. I leave you with this wonderful verse to remember, "Those who plant in tears will harvest with shouts of joy" (Psalm 126:5).

Chapter One

Who Are You and Who Do You Want to Be?

This is around my 1,890th day surviving post-divorce. It has not been easy! During my journey, it has felt as if I have been in a cave for many years where no one could see me—though I can see through such darkness and utter fog after what seemed to be an eternity of walking on eggshells. I have asked myself who I am *now* after all these days have passed, and the chips have finally fallen into their proper place. This question of who we are and who we are made to be is packed with so much information that I could be talking about it until the end of time. Instead, let me explain how I found my purpose and began living a more peaceful life by praying.

Praying, stillness, knowing my spiritual gifts, keeping my soul healthy, accepting vulnerabilities and shortcomings, and so much more! I propose that some of us may be unsteady in knowing ourselves after a devastating divorce; therefore, I believe this book is a great place to begin an incredible journey.

God gives us the Proverbs to help us know wisdom. They also

provide people with great value in balancing our goodness in doing the right thing; with the constant temptations of daily living. When a friend tells us, "I would not do that" or "Think wisely about that decision" it helps us to build more character and stand tall in who we are. We can gain strength in others with patience and humility if we are willing to listen. Thankfully, I had many wise voices of counsel during my divorce.

What Are Some Reasons We May Not Have Known Ourselves?

If we do not know ourselves, we may be suffering from a common issue that can be considered our blind spot. Two perfect examples are: we marry too young, or we may have never really gotten to know ourselves well enough before marriage. Due to these choices, we may not have experienced the level of life that we had always dreamed of. Or maybe we never dated enough to discover who the perfect fit for us is.

Once married, our lives may take many unexpected detours. The problem with detours is they change the trajectory of our journey. Meaning, the hope of a lasting marriage may not occur—it may end prematurely. Without great flexibility and maturity from both spouses, how does one handle the difficult struggles of marriage? I know that many women are dissatisfied with their marriages and know just as many men who feel the same way, too. Maybe dreams were never fulfilled, or traumatic events stole the normalcy of life that was once thought within reach. Husbands or wives soared on the corporate platform, leaving little opportunities for the other spouse to also have successful careers. Women need to be recognized and affirmed as homemakers while raising children.

Often women want quality time with their husbands, and it is innate and coded in our genetics. If we cannot articulate how to get affirmation and continued love once the spouse has become successful at work, then we feel left out or maybe abandoned. There are endless reasons why we are not happy and satisfied in our marriages. In this chapter, we will dive into our fundamental core to see a new, promising perspective.

I think we should start with an interesting and controversial theme, that has been going on since time began to uncover our true identities. Are we byproducts of nature or nurture? This is one of my favorite topics to discuss. Do you rely on the Holy Spirit for guidance in life or ourselves? Are you still open to hearing the voice of the Lord and following it? Do you allow God to mentor and help you make discerning decisions? Are you living under the power and authority of the Holy Ghost? If you're not listening to God's sovereign Word, you might be leading yourself down a road without hope and truth, living instead under the rules of what society is embracing at the time. When we follow the guidance of the Bible, we prosper in our maturity under God's law, not the law of man. There is so much more for us when we follow Christ.

Here is my approach to learning our true identities, to make it clear and simple. There are countless ways to break down what makes us tick and what we do and don't believe in. I propose it is a question of nature versus nurture. There are numerous renowned psychotherapists, like Sigmund Freud, who argued that our personalities are formed through nurture and environment. Early philosophers, like Plato and Descartes, suggest that we have genetics that occur inside us and form who we are to be. Then, to complicate things even more, another great mind, John Locke, believed that we are born with a clean slate and are to become who we are free of any inside static or genetic predisposition; this is more of an evolutionist viewpoint. These are ideas I learned through my years of experience in listening to clients discussing these many theories. So, what do we *really* all have in common?

1. We all have the image of God within us.
2. There is an invisible God, if you will, that creates order in our lives.
3. The Holy Spirit empowers us.

In the Bible, the apostle Paul speaks to this truth of God and how it affects us. There is so much power in the spiritual realm to the point it can seem scary, unnatural, or invigorating. We can dismiss or avoid this spiritual direction in our lives, but there is so much time spent forming our personalities before we are born. God is knitting our lives together before we can even conceptualize it.

Unfortunately, when we are hurt and so disappointed in life, we rely on seeing things in the natural realm instead of the spiritual realm. We tend to cling to what we can see and feel, but the spiritual realm can build us with greatness in our character, values, and morals through God. We are also creatures of instant gratification. This can lead us down a path we never thought we might cross. What many forget is that the nature side of things can be violent and cruel as well. Think of the winds, hurricanes, tornados, and other types of killings that we endure: it is the "survival of the fittest." Nature is where greed, power, and corruption of sin live. The constant war of life rages between the two forces of nature and nurture. This is where we can get abundantly lost and go to dark places, we may not have ever thought we would.

I believed, when I was first married, the person I thought that I knew was a man trying to follow a good path. The problem is we grew apart and became very different in a short amount of time. In a marriage, we can decide to either follow the goodness from being in God's image or not. When we are no longer guided by the Spirit, we fall upon our non-governed sinful natures. Hence, we hide sin just as Adam and Eve did in the Garden of Eden and hang out with others who are also keeping secrets from God and telling lies, just as Satan did. The ones who suffer the most from this behavior are our marital partners. Evil can see our blind spots! We know then what proceeds; secrets begin and ruin the heart, and passion and sinful desires take over. We forget to safeguard our souls and stay with people that affirm our faith and pull us back on track.

It is not easy to live a Godly and committed life outside of marriage or in marriage. We need to be taught and trained to execute the following: honor, avoiding the temptations of sexual immorality, and having never-ending respect for our partners. Furthermore, it is a necessity to have a solid accountability ring. That is why God explains the importance of rules and laws for us to be governed by in the Bible. Sinful nature eventually leads us to brokenness and suffering for those who have loved and trusted in us. Our personalities, if not equally yoked, take a detour because, if we are married as Christians, we are supposed to become one. Our personalities somehow supernaturally can mend together and make us stronger. Or tear us down exposing us to horrific sin and leading to the ultimate loss of faith in our partners and our marriages. Our willingness to follow the Holy Spirit or not helps determine the outcome.

Galatians 5:19-20 notes examples of horrible sins: "Sexual immorality, impurity, lustful pleasures, idolatry, sorcery, hostility, quarreling, jealousy, outbursts of anger, selfish ambition, dissension, division, envy, drunkenness, wild parties, and other sins like these."

Wow, is that enough to make you feel like we have daily uphill journeys to face in resisting temptations and need to tighten our armor of God a little more? I understand in many ways why husbands, and wives, change so much in life, and not always for the better. The pressure from constant societal push can easily invade our values if we are not in constant peace with God. Society is constantly trying to push individuals into a new way of acceptance or thinking. I feel that our society has grown very liberal, leaving little space for true family values to flourish. We need to safeguard our souls. We can never allow a gap to stretch because we will eventually fall in. Sometimes change is so subtle we do not even notice it until we are knee-deep and the guilt begins to overflow. This is where a true destruction zone can be a pitfall in our life. I lived it firsthand in my marriage, and it was not fun to be able to see it so clearly while others had their eyes wide shut.

I think God removed me from the temptations that come with many big corporate jobs, enticing money opportunities, and the trajectory of becoming a workaholic. This could have been easy for me before, during, and after getting married. Maybe God wanted more in my life and made room for it through marriage and having a family. I could rely on God more, and hear and follow the Holy Spirit clearer, without all the noise of my career. However, I have seen men and women fall and crumble in their marriages and relationships based on a lack of quality time and intimacy because of never-ending work. I believe a spouse can leave in the morning for work and come home to a slightly different person in the afternoon, having little interest or time to understand what is going on with their partner or family.

In my experience, I remember getting further and further apart from my husband until I woke up and felt like his roommate instead of his wife. I no longer could recognize the man that I married. I also know what it is like for that same person to not come home and refuse to explain their whereabouts. It is crushing, but you must stay true to your character and not let your personality waiver. There is a choice to make; that is deciding whether to follow your spouse down a road leading to more destruction or not. Know you can trust God during this difficult time and remember that He never leaves us (Galatians 5:24).

I am so grateful God has protected me and kept me from the sexual immorality, pornography, addiction, and lustful living that befall others. He has been so generous to me in that regard. I try to stay away and remove myself from these afflictions and addictions so that I can move forward and keep in step on my journey of faith. This is not to say that anger and outbursts did not occur from me during my marriage, but I knew big changes needed to happen to avoid other temptations. My anger and frustration was in direct alignment to protecting my marriage.

Interestingly, the power of unforeseen pressures in dire situations can temporarily change you, leading to a struggling relationship. I recognized something was wrong in my marriage that affected my moods, and my inner consciousness was trying to warn me of this irregularity. Why did I feel like I needed to constantly defend myself in continuous arguments over the smallest things with my former husband? God is the only person that I need to answer to. I felt like I was on trial for many days and finally gave up the battle.

All I can say is that, as an everyday person and believer, I did not know myself well enough. Furthermore, I did not know my full identity in God. This could have eased and overcome the pain of the sin I saw before me. I could not seem to change or alter the problems in my marriage no matter what I suggested. However, I can have empathy for those I know who struggled with the desires of the heart. I believe many people constantly are chasing power in their jobs, sex, money, and more control. I suspect they are quite empty at the end of their lives after all that chasing and pursuing nothing that can truly make them happy. This begs the next question.

Why do we rarely ask ourselves, "Who are we really and how do we stay on the straight and narrow, embracing life as God intended?" As a therapist, grasping this knowledge is so important that I have every client of mine take several quizzes upon hiring me. I believe to fully interact with others is to know all about a client's strengths and weaknesses. It allows for optimum understanding and healthier communication between a therapist and a client and a client with others.

Additionally, knowing who you are may help in knowing your blind spots in life. Have you ever wondered about how an individual, in a passionate moment, can severely hurt their spouse and wind up in court or, worse, prison? We think that we know ourselves, but so many intricate details and flaws are hard to handle at some levels in our personalities. There is also the factor of mental illness. Some of us can break mentally after certain circumstances are put upon us such as job loss, parental and family deaths, and pressures from ungodly people demanding our attention until it leads to our demise. I want to believe that most people want and need to feel loved and fulfilled in life. This awareness of great intimacy can be so joyful when it is finally experienced. The pinnacle of connection is a great need among us as well.

If it is our goal to avoid hurtful pitfalls, and unhealthy relationships, and find quality in our authentic selves, then I generally begin with *The 5 Love Language Quiz* and the *16 Personality Quiz*, both of which are free, easy to complete, and can be found online (See Toolbox).

These essential testing tools not only give us valuable information about our inner selves, but they also assist in foretelling whether or not two individuals might be compatible in a relationship. Moreover, these instruments can easily assist us in really getting to know ourselves down to our cores. A better equipped *you* embraces other's weaknesses with mercy and grace instead of disgust and anguish. Just for a moment, imagine the benefits of knowing oneself perfectly or authentically. This inner knowledge is worth more than any gift of intuition or any counseling master's program can teach.

I have admired author Leslie Vernick and her book, *The Emotionally Destructive Marriage*. The author has a quiz at the beginning of her book that is very enlightening, helping discern the state of your marriage and assisting a person's journey toward understanding types of marital abuse. I highly recommend this book as a good read to help support you with resources.

Since life's journey is just as complex as we are as humans, it is also important to understand what other factors affect our personalities. Do you know if you are divergent or non-divergent? Many have never heard of these terms, so I will explain them. Some people grow up in a rather perfect environment, with parents who never get a divorce, have little financial issues, and certainly don't have traumas to report. This would be our so-called normal, non-divergent group.

Others have more issues to compete with such as being diagnosed on the spectrum, persistent depression, post-traumatic stress, anxiety, and so many more. We could become adults and one day find out we have attention deficit disorder (ADD), which changes many things in how we navigate life. This is considered part of the divergent group. It is vitally important we know these facts about our mental health before entering relationships. It can be a very risky engagement when your partner does not understand you and is your opposite, living as a person never exposed to a mental illness. I call them non-divergent individuals.

The more that pressure reigns down on us, the more opportunity we have to observe the frailty in the world that exists among us. We can be reactive to these situations, causing our life journeys to spin in seconds. God's teaching of the fruit of the Spirit, and how to cultivate it, can be the center of your training grounds for these pressures and situations. Make sure the husband you choose to marry can empower you as a leader to express your godly gift and stand with you in these pressures. It's something I believe many women desire but seldom speak of. A man lacking leadership in his husband's role cannot always see God's many examples of guidance. Therefore, many marriages are lacking the undertaking of authentically knowing their word and accountability.

I believe that when we are faced with difficulties, many of us can realize just how brave and powerful we are. We sometimes may need to tweak our personalities and pull out the hidden gifts of patience, kindness, humility, and wisdom, but we all can help and empower others. Humility is my favorite attribute, putting pride in the backseat. Some of my favorite Bible verses concerning this matter of humility are (Proverbs 11:2, Proverbs 16:5, v. 18)

While this is a very difficult virtue (losing pride and gaining humility) to maintain, we can unlearn bad habits just as much as we are capable of learning great ones. Acquiring support, from God and others, to allow us to grow in our journeys can change our pathways. When we embrace as many resources as possible from God, we can make better decisions. Remember, happiness and stability will follow. One of my favorite authors is Brené Brown. She has a variety of books with some wise words on courage and bravery for women starting over. I recommend her books to those who are looking for support for life after divorce.

It is important to embrace the goodness of life's blessings with our world constantly changing but to also be wise in recognizing that increasing dissent is also separating us as a united front. This very point goes right back to "Who are you?" Are you steadfast in your beliefs, regardless of the changing tone of politics, sexuality, and trends that go in and out? Or are you a chameleon and want to be accepted so badly that you change your stance at any moment in time? I see the division amongst us growing with the increased usage of social media platforms and other media outlets to share our differing opinions. There are daily measures of dissension we experience, and it is powerful.

Anger is another part of knowing yourself, which can be lethal without great prayer and constant checks and balances of your personality. I think this totality of such rage and loss during this time in history (2020-2022) has created isolation and disengaged us from our society to such an extent that the level of rising mental illness in anxiety and depression finally hit a publicly-noticed toll, especially for marriages.

Another facet of knowing thy self is accepting you may have a mental illness if you are diagnosed with one. The existence of mental illness has been documented since our ancestors, the Greeks, were alive. In 1883, the German psychiatrist Emil Kräpelin (1856–1926) published something that changed the world, a highly detailed system of psychological disorders that centered around a pattern of symptoms. I often wonder how we live in the twenty-first century, and only now mental illness is becoming recognized as an acceptable illness to be openly discussed. Television commercials with popular sports athletes, musicians, and Hollywood actors are speaking out about mental health. Our government is beginning to understand that mental health needs to be recognized, and people need help in navigating such illnesses without fear of the negative connotation limiting their treatment.

From November 1874 to January 1965, a British statesman, soldier, and writer named Winston Churchill[ii], Prime Minister of the United Kingdom at the time, stated, "Fear is a reaction. Courage is a decision." It is ever so true. The ongoing pandemic from 2020 to 2022 changed so many people's lives. Parents were home more to watch and notice their children's development while marriages that were on the brink of disaster either reached for help or faltered to their end.

During 2020–2023, COVID-19, the constant distancing and absence of socialization in school, work, and play took a toll on us all. This is because fear can either paralyze people, increase anger, or motivate us to a higher level of determination to survive. This season of handling COVID-19, and the havoc it wreaked on the world, led many people down a road of dissension.

It was a season plagued not only with unbelievably high statistics of deaths but rising divorce rates. The divorce rates were mostly caused by couples being at home instead of working. Some were let go from jobs they had for many years. Others were forced to take a vaccine to keep their jobs. Many changes took place that were both good and bad. While some people became more focused on helping others, others looked for anyone else to blame for their anger and loneliness. The news highlighted for many months the dangers of the virus and embraced a pattern of hopelessness and hatred from city to city. This puts pressure on any person married or not. Changes that we cannot control and did not see coming are shocking and stressful at best.

However, a person mentored well by others is a person who is confident in their self and their abilities. They can become like a well-oiled machine and capable of wonderful things, as well-minded people spread wellness and hope to others when they feel this wellness inside.

Sometimes we are influenced by uncontrollable situations and unforeseen events. These experiences make it more difficult to know our inner selves. I guess in some ways we ignore our need for adjustment, but I'd like to believe that most of us want to be our "best selves" and find inner peace. By embracing the identity of God in us, we can see ourselves. This takes constant rehearsal just as a person might do before a large presentation or as a musician may do before going on a world tour. This may take constant tweaking of ourselves to maintain a version of our best selves, as there must be room for improvement for most of us.

For those people who never adjust, they stay stuck. They ruminate constantly on negativity and the past. This type of person may never truly know themselves in their endurance, tolerance, and ability to improve. Except for narcissists, I think there is a tremendous value in needing to improve ourselves, like a car tune-up every so often. On a spiritual level, some of us have lost hope and have trouble believing we can make society whole again. This thinking may warrant some truth if comparing some of history's most horrific tragedies to one another. We can also pose a question if society is capable of turning its back on one another, then what standard do we have in society to save marriages and prevent couples from turning their backs on one another?

This is an interesting dilemma of good versus evil in general. This very concept questions many regarding their faith in God and His plans for marriage. I still remember in graduate school, one of my professors had us write an essay on the idea of "Do we believe that we are born with a desire to be good, or do we have a preset behavior toward evil?" I want to believe we are all born good; however, I think we struggle to be good and do the right things in life. My paper was a struggle to complete but opened a new world of thinking for me.

My faith tells me that even though we are born into a world of sin, we can still have the ability to recognize honor, and self-control to become loving and forgiving people. I do not believe being "loving" is easy. However, the more we know our hearts and our willingness to strengthen them, the more we become empathic toward others' needs. I think God gives all of us a purpose, and when engaged, that purpose naturally promotes gentleness and lovingness toward our neighbors. This compassion can continue from generation to generation, not only in individuals but also in couples in marriages.

A Milestone to Knowing One's Self

Abraham Maslow, an esteemed American psychologist, is known for his famous five basic hierarchy triangle of needs: psychological, safety, belonging, love, prestige, and, at the highest level, the need for self-actualization. I believe self-actualization is where some put themselves first above others. The upside of self-actualization is achieving one's highest potential, while the downside is an unhealthy example of narcissism, a mental illness listed in *The Diagnostic and Statistical Manual of Mental Disorders, 5th Edition*[iii].

Maslow's Hierarchy of Needs

As seen above, certain people are better than others at reaching self-actualization. It is narrow at the top for a reason. Narcissists and power-driven individuals are commonly excellent at this though it is achieved at another's cost (see Chapter 4). They tend to thrive on others' success only when it is tethered back to their success. Obviously, between the upside and downside of self-actualization, there are several stages to go through for a person.

There are so many unanticipated ups and downs in a marriage, but the sickness of a personality flaw, such as being narcissistic, takes a toll and can be mind-bending to a partner. Many believe this personality disorder most likely cannot be reckoned with as they always want to be in control and desire the limelight to appear perfect and charming. Not many people ever get close enough to narcissists, due to their need for perfection, competition, and success. This narcissistic trait is common among those on the end of self-actualization; most are erratic about the truth they believe.

Who Do You Want to Be?

Lou Tzu, an Ancient Chinese philosopher and founder of Taoism said, "If you are depressed, you are living in the past. If you are anxious, you are living in the future. If you are at peace, you are living in the present." I love this quote used as a baseline for some people, but certainly not all people. It does make us think though about what we are doing in life. I believe that all of us need a life purpose statement of what we believe and stand for that is connected to our values. This personal statement encompasses who we are, who we want to be, and our strengths, talents, and level of perseverance. It took me years of revising my personal life statement so that it was authentic. Now, I have it to my perfection hopefully for many years to come. Here it is:

"To motivate and inspire others to live a life where they are mentally and physically healthy, and have peace and contentment. To hear God's calling and trust Him to follow His wisdom and share my story with others who may be wavering in their faith."

Self-love is a very important component of knowing who you are. If you cannot love yourself then how can you love others? I like to think that as a Christian, it is easier to love ourselves. We are a true miracle. God's love is the highest form of love. It can fill us when we are down. It never runs out. This love gives us eternal hope that others may need to experience. To stay healthy, our self-love needs a checkup every once in a while.

Certain types of people truly do not care nor can genuinely love others. They enjoy the thrill of mentally hurting and destroying them. This type of person learns how to perfectly gaslight the ones they know love them. This is a term that is often used in divorce cases and is linked with narcissistic behavior. We cannot be subjected to this behavior. When we give someone trust, not worthy of your trust, you give them the power to destroy you. This harms us on so many levels. With *proper* self-love and the support of others, this should never be a factor in our journey.

Self-love cannot compete with narcissistic behaviors. Too often, those who are narcissistic believe that their wants and needs matter first ahead of their spouse's or anyone else. If the spouse does not agree with the point of view or opinion of a narcissist, then the narcissist orchestrates disturbing behaviors in relationships, creates calculated painful divorces, purposely asks for forgiveness later, and can never see beyond their sabotaging agendas. They can cause insurmountable, emotional damage and pain to others in life, especially during the divorce process. These actions can make a person feel isolated, guilty, and lost. A person is not built for this hatred. It changes us and leaves us with an emptiness inside. We cannot see ourselves clearly as we are. We lose the ability to know ourselves and it is really hard work to put ourselves back together. This emotional upheaval leaves scars deeper than a hornet's poisonous sting and great emptiness for their partners.

I survived twenty-one years in a marriage where my identity was often called into question. I became very confused about who I was and my purpose in life. I lived with a twisted view of happiness and stability. Looking back, I think my mind was not able to handle the conflicting view of what I thought my marriage was. I started seeing the truth about our marriage and the absence of God. It was difficult for me to reconcile what I had trusted about my marriage—which for over a decade may have once been true but it was the exception, not the rule. That loss of that ideal was so damaging to me, and there are many women (men too) who have suffered from the same delusion in their marriages. The past emotional wreckage that women and men undergo during this process of knowing who we married is very traumatizing to the soul. My complex post-traumatic stress disorder (PTSD) began during my marriage and got worse during the divorce. It has changed my view on stability and trust in others. I pray for God's help daily to reverse what happened so that I can be the person He intended me to be. PTSD makes us lose our trust in our authentic selves. There are many ways to recover from this with God's help and good intervention.

So, are you getting a better picture in determining who you are? Can you clear your mind after deprived relationships and get to a healthier baseline to reboot again? Does your subconscious mind play a part in the consciousness of your decisions, especially regarding marriage? Think about these deep, reflective questions before getting married, especially if you have already been married once and are now considering a second marriage. Be sure that if you have ears to hear, the ability to listen, and an open mind, you can be guided by the Spirit toward the unfolding of goodness in your life. God wants us to embrace our marriages as being each other's eternal helpmates, not wolves dressed in sleep's clothing who are hungry to deceive and destroy.

Recognize all the pieces of the puzzle that make up your DNA, thus your personality. Suffering is just one part of who we are and who we become. It is impossible to escape while you are alive. Suffering can help us grow in many ways we may not always comprehend, both good and bad, even though the Bible speaks of suffering in a very positive light. How do we get to our best selves? We can start by looking for others who understand the worth and value of one another as well as understand the importance of becoming more unified in helping each other understand our worth. Have you ever noticed why you prefer one friend's company over another's? Generally, it is because they nurture our souls and encourage our understanding of life in a manner we can grasp.

Life is not easy to navigate, and some days it seems impossible. I still remember working in the emergency room as an inpatient trauma specialist and witnessing the aftermaths of many graphic suicide attempts, while listening to many stories of hopelessness from some patients. I think about those people I met and how their turmoil will be forever written in my heart, me personally and spiritually. As I learn about myself through life experiences, both good and bad, my struggles seem to help me to assimilate the importance of being kind to others. My power is in showing up to comfort and encourage others, and myself in the process, during the hardest times.

My story of surviving the hardest times began when my son in-utero was diagnosed with an insurmountable, deadly condition, which led local hospitals with geneticists and other important staff to advise against my pregnancy and deem my pregnancy not to be salvageable. My dreams and hopes of being a mother died in a matter of seconds as all I was hearing were the negative, tragic, and hard-to-grasp medical reasons as to why the pregnancy should be terminated. I originally went to the doctor believing I had kidney stones. I went from finding out that I did not have kidney stones to hearing that I was having a baby. Then, I learned I was having twins. The hospital staff tried to educate me that my pregnancy would be a burden to society long-term due to the baby's potential adsorbent disabilities.

At that moment, it became clear that my lonely marriage journey would challenge my new emotional motherhood journey. I have always been a fighter and known to be strong by my friends.

No one ever can see inside our heads which is a good thing, I reckon. Even when someone swears that they know your most intimate thoughts, this cannot be the truth. The amount of pain and suffering I learned in those nine months, and then three years after the birth of my baby, taught me nothing short of true devotion and great motherly character. I guess that is when I decided I needed to get to know myself better. I never thought I would have made it to this point when all the odds seemed against me, but I have a story to share with others about such sadness, internal struggle, and courage in hardship. Begin with learning your true north and divine purpose.

Toolbox 1:
- Are you a product of nature or nurture or a pleasant combination?
- One hour a week at church is not enough to foster goodness in your heart or mind. It requires stable leadership and guidance to keep your character sharp. Praying, reading the Bible, going to church more, and fasting are ways to sharpen your character.
- Know who is close to your husband in the business environment. Understanding the lies and other manipulating techniques by desperate women to gain the attention of your husband is crucial. The *Damsel-in-Distress Syndrome* is a great attention-catcher to break up marriages for men with low self-esteem wanting the hero complex attention.
- When you give trust someone unworthy of your trust you give them the power to destroy you.
- You cannot escape suffering in this life. But you can come out the other side better by changing your perspective on your situation of frustration, stress, and awfulness.
- You can find triumph in this difficult journey. When you feel trapped by your enemies, understand God is in the outer circle at all times protecting you.

- Listen to others in your life who have wise counsel to share with you. This will build your character strong.
- When in doubt read the book of Proverbs because when we face difficulties and are suffering, we can realize just how brave and powerful we are by tuning into the voice and guidance of the Holy Spirit and Word of God.
- Devote some prayer time to help you see who you are meant to be.
- You can learn to know yourself well with a desired interest to improve and work on yourself with various assessments, (as seen on Resources page).

Chapter Two

Who Teaches Us Commitment and What Does It Really Mean to Us?

I am writing this book from my own experiences within the modern-day world. That is not to say I am perfectly aware of the latest culture and beliefs. I believe many in their high school and college years of the new generation of selfishness and pride. I am not so sure how society's children changed so much. I do believe that many viewpoints today have misplaced values. Maybe one day, this will be recognized and overturned.

I think children of my generation (1980–1990s) regarded our parents and grandparents' authority at the highest level. We watched closely at how parents engaged because family meant so much to us. Previous wars and the perishing of lives were still threats. I don't remember myself or my friends ever insulting, degrading, fighting, or losing contact with their parents—which no longer holds today, and I am witness to it. These characteristics affect commitment across the board. I watch how relationships are disposable in high school and college students today through 2014-2023—concerned that it may lead to diminished marriages for our future generation. How sad. I always told my son to watch how girlfriends treat their parents and watch what you choose to do with girlfriends. They will be wives one day. Protect women to be pure and holy.

Now, pretending to be a good man or husband and being one are two very different realities. The same pretense goes for wives. Years of living with someone does not guarantee their loyalty or long-term commitment. Commitment is nothing short of truly understanding your faith and divine purpose because not many other things trump this. Commitment in a marriage versus a privation of commitment is likely to result in a destructive relationship and possible divorce. After treating hundreds of clients in my profession, I have listened to many stories about relationship loss and grief due to a lack of commitment. Gaining insight into surviving a broken commitment will enhance your ability to heal and recover successfully. Some of my advice may seem like common sense to some, but complex and confusing for others. That is why insight from others can be valuable.

Commitment and faith in God have two things in common: constant growth and determination. Faith has guided me through my only marital relationship, with God lifting the insurmountable pain from me. I probably know myself better now and have maintained my commitment to Christ, never wavering during my divorce's trauma. My marriage was never thriving. Instead, it was lacking life since the beginning.

Ten years into the marriage was still hopeless. My son brought great joy to me and helped me manage a loveless marriage. I am grateful that one good thing came from my 22 years of marriage. God knows us better than anyone on this earth. I never forget that He is our Father and gives us good things. He opened a unique door for me to see hope again. I understand now that certain situations must occur for goodness to happen again and for doors of blessing to open.

After my divorce, forgiveness and God's supernatural power were the most intense feelings I experienced. I am here to tell you the light is at the end of the divorce tunnel. God gives us beautiful things and can take them away at any moment. This truth does not have to be perceived as unfavorable, just a way to live in the moment and be grateful for the things that may not have permanence in our lives.

After any devastating storm in a relationship, some may agree that the finality of a broken commitment may be a blessing in disguise. The key to emerging with a new, hopeful vantage point is to arise from the depths of a divorce and its battlefield instead of staying in it. We can regain acceptance of our value once we escape the memories of our damaged selves, which divorce can replay constantly. Just for a moment, believe in commitment again. With great determination, you will learn to see the truth about yourself again as you continue believing in loyalty.

For many reasons, some of us can grow closer to God through relationship storms, but others can become weaker and lose faith in God. Stressful times separate many of us from God's side because we cannot understand how God allows suffering. We forget the power and greatness of free will, and that free will means God gives us the chance to make good and bad choices. For myself, God had a covering over me like an umbrella and wrapped the broken pieces of my soul in a blanket during my divorce, even when I feared that He could not help. He continually gave me hope, stability, and peace when I prayed for healing from my broken marital commitment.

Here are two profound questions about commitment. How is commitment so interwoven with knowing ourselves? Does personal willpower or commitment overshadow who we are, or is it just an obligation? We will undoubtedly lack the willpower to sustain significant commitment if we are weak-minded. Without steadfast commitment, we are nothing of value to others. Isn't commitment a true sign of devout love? Developing commitment is nothing short of being a great role model as a mother or father to your children. In my marriage, I was never accompanied by my husband kneeling nor praying together out loud for my son to witness or anyone else. This missing component was paralyzing and baffling to me how a so-called Christian family did not cherish the opportunity to strengthen their bond as a family and honor God. This factor led to the eventual loss of viewing my husband as a leader of our home. My former husband was not the committed husband I had prayed for many years before marriage.

Marriage and praying for what you desire can be two very different things. It can challenge every fiber in your body. I value loyalty in marriage as a synonym for commitment. Do you wonder if you would stay in your marriage if an accident happened to your spouse and they became paralyzed? Would you stay if your husband was a good salesman and acted like a true believer, but he was never really that person behind closed doors? What if a stronghold came over your husband and wreaked havoc? Would you be patient and stay? What if you had a young child that saw and heard terrible things about you from your spouse or his family? These circumstances happen more often than one might think and can test our commitment levels to each other in marriage.

Commitment is like our baseline in determining and uncovering who we are and how faithful we remain in all things. In my marriage, there was no equal balance and sacrifice; therefore, the commitment never stood on a true promise. It seemed more like an obligation to be together, even though I greatly desired to make our marriage work. I had great hope for 22 years that our marriage could have a reckoning. Although this never came to pass, and the price tag on my physical and mental health grew steadily. I lived with a $22,000 debt from Emory Hospital (my health insurance lapsed) due to a heart condition; while being part of the hospital, I had often walked the halls as an employee once before. I knew this lifestyle of worry and sadness after divorce must come to a final ending, or my health would end me.

While I would never wish this experience on anyone, it was an excellent wake-up call. I wanted more people to value commitment as I still do. Maybe believers and non-believers could view sound commitments as a healthier way of life. What an incredible thought that marriages could be unbreakable. I read this quote and have made it a daily routine of mine. Bruce Lee stated, "Do not pray for an easy life; pray for the strength to endure a difficult one."

Our inner identity mirrors our values and beliefs, guiding who we want to be. We all have spiritual gifts and natural talents; some choose to use them while others do not. My strength is to help others seek wisdom and discernment while understanding proper and healthy relationship boundaries. This gift allows others to better cultivate positivity through being at peace with whatever life throws at them, thus making them more committed individuals in life in general. Sometimes the gratitude and mercy we want is something we only see after the commitment breaks. However, God provides a window for us to finally see truth during our time of deprivation, like being in a desert without water and seeing an oasis on the horizon. God allows us to know the value of others through their commitment to us.

I hope to provide you with many valuable skills to put into your life toolbox (yes, you need one) for a rainy day to manage yourself during trying times. I want you to see the truth, commitment, and fantastic value in this world. I am sure you have heard that when one door shuts, a new door opens. I want to help you discover the open doors and the next journey of light. Shut the window, lock it, and when necessary, you may continue God's intended voyage for you through a new open door or window.

It should be second nature to protect yourself and have a level of fear about the unknown, commitment, relationships, and marriages. But it is crucial to have a sense of balanced protection and not a zipper bag filled with feelings of overwhelming fear and anxiety. How do we know the right amount of love in a relationship? Is there a perfect recipe for genuine commitment? The following chapters will help you understand this process.

A Piece of Knowing Thyself: Being Authentic

Many women and men do not know themselves authentically, especially after divorce. They become messy and unbalanced. It is somewhat bewildering—to function well in a sound relationship and hold commitment, we women must love ourselves first. Do not become confused about who you are. So many women are in co-dependent and sometimes abusive relationships for various reasons. One of those reasons is that some women don't truly understand why two people come together as one in a commitment. Some women stay in marriages because they are lost spiritually and not committed to their marriages with God in the center of the marriage. Others have forgotten a healthy perspective on marriage with proper boundaries, and not because they aren't committed. You can choose to be committed to your marriage or non-committal in relationships. Knowing yourself well makes it easier to tell whether you're committed.

God gives us strength to overcome most things we thought were impossible. Proverbs 31:25 states, "She is clothed with strength and dignity; she can laugh at the days to come." And John 16:33 says, "I have told you these things, so that in me you may have peace. In this world, you will have trouble. But take heart! I have overcome the world."

Commitment is still required after a marriage is over. We are mothers and protectors of our children; that is a divine commitment, not simply broken. When God blesses mothers with children, it is a special gift and a lifetime promise. Suppose parents do not act on the ability to encourage faithful, long-lasting relationships with their children. How can the child grow up with a knowledge of and respect toward a commitment to others? Poor role modeling can cause remorse, lack of empathy, and poor understanding of commitment for some children, resulting in relational avoidance and diminished love. Let's be honest; if a mother and father cannot show positive, nurturing, and loving behavior toward one another, how can their children grow up to nurture their marriages and children with greatness?

"But if you cause little ones who trust in me to fall into sin, it would be better for you to be thrown into the sea with a large millstone hung around your neck." Mark 9:42

Parenting and Commitment

Parenting comes with significant responsibilities—some people are good at it, while others wreak havoc and cause destruction for their growing children. Their behavior only perpetuates the lack of commitment in them. In many cases, one or both immature parents likely lacked the tools and skills to uphold boundaries, morals, and values from their dysfunctional home lives. The cycle continues like an addictive behavior as both go into marriage.

We can stay strong and show our children what commitment is made of. We can be rugged outliers. We can purge the thoughts and actions that crush commitment. Reflect goodness in your parenting, and you will later see the fruitfulness. Side note: this is an excellent time to introduce duplicity or my thoughts on splitting. Are you the same person on the inside and outside? Do you reflect in a mirror and stay true to who you think you are? Do you gossip about others and secretly sexually desire someone who has caught your eye? Have you forgotten you have a spouse and children?

Duplicity allows one to do things that no one saw coming, including themselves. The person that they said they never wanted to be is who they are becoming. The problem is that they do not know what has happened. It is like scales have covered their eyes. They may never see what destruction in their family lives and other lives they have destroyed until judgment day with our Maker. God cannot make us wrong; only we are capable of this.

We Are All in Training

Growing up, I learned mistakes meant I was not paying precise attention, lacked commitment, or laziness. I started to think something might be wrong with me because focusing seemed so complicated. I felt great embarrassment and confusion, which contradicted my faith that God made me perfect to Him. I felt shameful that I did not have the same interest and devotion in school as others. I was a misfit for some time in school.

I remember having a few exceptional teachers in high school and college. They helped me see that their commitment to teaching was an honor. I experienced the outpouring of love and extra conversations about personal direction from several of them during hard times with my family. Their attentiveness is another part of shaping my idea of what commitment would look like.

When I earned my first master's degree, I no longer believed I lacked focus; instead, I knew what commitment was. Only through significant commitment was I able to finish my degree while preparing for my divorce. I still remember inviting some of my family I had not seen for years to my graduation ceremony. My husband stated, "Anyone can get a master's degree; what is the big deal?" Those words sliced through me, and I showed my son that I was courageous and could complete my commitment to finishing my degree even under great duress. I tried to be a good role model to my son. Divorce can almost rip your soul out; it does not need to define, kill, or lower your standard of being a good mother.

I learned commitment in my family through our Catholic faith. Growing up Catholic, my family was committed to church on Sundays and holidays. We also were dedicated to regularly confessing our sins. I tried to avoid going to confession at all costs because it made me feel like such a terrible child, teen, and then adult. I often wondered if everyone in the church had similar feelings about themselves before confession. Going to confession was not a commitment that I wanted to continue.

Sometime in college, I decided to take control of my thoughts about commitment and merge that with my belief in great character. We can control our character growth with great promise as soon as we begin making commitments we intend to keep. Doing so honors our authentic selves and God as we start our journeys in the authenticity of how we are and who we want to become.

When destructive and non-committal people get in our way, we feel less than whole. It can be tormenting and do real damage to our self-esteem and faith. But listen, that is only if we allow it, and I understand there are always exceptions. Please know that you do not need to take abuse at any time. You have such power within yourself, so reach inside and learn to use it. I waited too long to use mine and beat myself up for undeserving thoughts that raced through my head. Embrace your culture and family traditions to help you determine your strength and direction in life. Commitment has a connection within your soul and heritage.

Culture and Commitment

I am an Italian woman and love the tradition of being with my family and having good food and hospitality for my friends. My favorite dishes growing up were spaghetti and meatballs, and lasagna. Those are happy memories for me on Sundays after church going to my grandmother's house and having a homemade meal to share with my family. My two aunts and both grandmothers are very special to me. It was hard for me when my grandmother passed away because I was only thirteen and then fifteen at each passing time. I never really got to know these godly women as well as I had wished.

While trying to learn the many life teachings as a teen, I felt stripped of two people who seemed to love me very much. The security and love they offered me made me feel special and gave me purpose. On the other hand, my self-esteem seemed to drop a few notches as I wrestled with their deaths. The loss was affecting my inner being while challenging me to be strong. However, I consider the loss of a hostile entity that robs our joy by stealing people from us without warning. Here is when I began to struggle with understanding how helpless our hearts are in dealing with these situations of pure sadness; hence, depression and anxiety can start to creep in. I had not experienced loss until that moment in time and would have thought that these losses might have prepared me for the loss of my marriage. Unfortunately, it did not, and the pain was still insufferable.

My journey in divorce began with an awakening to evaluate

my deepest values, morals, and character. It made me wonder how other people without faith can handle grief, loss, and broken commitment. This thought begs the question: when we are married for an extended number of years, who are we when our spouses leave us? Do we still have a genuine and clear picture of who we are now and who we will become after a divorce? That is why it is essential that we truly know ourselves thoroughly before joining in an engagement or marriage.

For this reason, I will give you my position on departing a relationship and going through a divorce. I believe divorce is necessary for extreme or abusive situations. I do not think getting a divorce should be absolute when one spouse has fallen out of love with the other or is in love with another or when there is a seeming incapability to get along. God has spoken so many times on restoration in His Word (Psalms 51:12; 1 Peter 5:10; Jeremiah 30:17). How can we be silent or proud in hearing this teaching?

I recently listened to a podcast from Victory Church in Atlanta, Georgia, where the pastor gave a sermon on marriage and family. It was so powerful that it brought tears to my eyes. The general message was never to leave a foothold for the devil to invade your marriage. As a nation and society, we have been forced to allow our ears and eyes to hear and see things that God did not intend. We often cannot protect ourselves quickly enough from imminent danger in our marriages. We become desensitized from what goodness has been designed for us and the privileges of marriage and parents. We are role models that little ones see, so how do we stand tall in a much-fallen world? It seems exhausting to think about, but God knew this and heeded a warning about these dangers in His Word.

"But if you do not do what is right, watch out because sin is crouching at the door, ready to pounce on you! You must master it before it masters you." Genesis 4:7

I think there is a pain many of us are meant to experience here on earth so that we can uncover more answers about ourselves. After getting married, I learned things about myself that I never could have predicted. If you lean into faith, it will sustain you through the darkest moments imaginable. I woke up many nights afraid of the future of my marriage as the hate in my home brought me to pure exhaustion. My husband and I disagreed during our marriage about the faith in which to raise our child, and I could not persuade him otherwise. He would not agree to a supportive Bible study for him which I felt would teach our son about character and commitment that I knew could help him in his future. He needed a good mentor and support system as the divorce began.

It would be best to extend your comforting wing as a mother and always protect your children, no matter what happens in your marriage. Bring up your children well with compassion and love for all things. Have them understand there is no shame in offering apologies and tenderness. Let forgiveness be the mortar or filling that binds your family's legacy. And let no person poison your family, leading to separation or divorce. Many personal experiences have helped me better understand the wicked struggles of other mothers living similar travesties through divorce.

I can deeply relate to the many clients who admitted that anxiety and panic attacks had become a new diagnosis after divorce. So many are on various medications to soften the blow of divorce so they can still function and continue working and providing for their children. Other mothers have shared with me that thoughts of suicide were closer to a reality for them than they ever imagined during the divorce process. As wives and mothers, we are tender, sensitive, and firm. Our empathy and constant commitment help raise little children into excellent future fathers, mothers, husbands, and wives. While ultimately believing that our children will echo back our efforts in pure nurturing to their children.

I wanted to believe that my marriage would have excellent protection against evil and sin for all the years of my life. I imagined growing old and having our son with us on birthdays, holidays, breaks from college, his wedding day, and the birth of his children. However, this idea has been stolen from me forever because of my divorce, and I am left with only memories. There won't be any more memory-making on special days together. I have already lost precious time as a mother watching, alone, my son experiences so many important days of his life since the divorce, and I still wrestle with the profound loss in my mind and soul. I still stand in my son's room and wonder what it would have been like to watch him grow each day, to see his expressions as his maturity deepened.

Divorce was never an option for me until my former husband served me and later forced me to sign 21 years of my life away and bury my commitment to Christ that I had made kneeling at an altar in his church home. After signing so many documents, some expected and others unexpected, with secretive and confidential information. This process has prevented me from being authentic in many ways and staying true to my commitment to marriage even when it was deteriorating my health. If I could redo signatures, I would have refused to sign many agreements regarding my divorce and pushed more to work on my marriage. It forced me to forever be in an unwanted category of "the divorced," making me feel less than and like a failure at commitment which I valued so highly.

The church and my family taught me that marriage is a sacrament. Therefore, divorce diminished my ability to remain sacred and compromised my values. I now wholeheartedly understand how some women get pushed aside after a nasty divorce and the negativity surrounding them for what seems like an eternity. Like a scarlet letter, it is almost as though a woman carries the burden of shame and embarrassment forever.

Divorce was, sadly, in my family as one of my grandmothers was a divorcee in the 1950s, and her quality of life was never the same after. I believe that she suffered tremendously from this loss. She never remarried and lived a short life. My other grandmother stayed married until her death.

My mother's parents divorced early in their marriage after my grandfather fell in love with another woman. It was sad not only for my mother but for all her siblings. Unfortunately, this lack of commitment in marriages can have such an effect on a family. I would have never believed it would have trickled down to me as a grandchild. The sense of safety, true love, and honor in a Christian marriage have been complex to fathom, finding myself also divorced. Relationships ending is a devastating experience that may decrease future commitment. When a person has no choice but to break their marital vows with their spouse, what does that say about genuine commitment?

I remember my parents were happy when I was young; they seemed like the perfect couple and probably were. My parents were both beautiful and handsome. Many people were in awe of them. We had awesome Christmases and family vacations and seemed close. My dad was successful in business in executive management, and my mother also enjoyed her career as a hairstylist, beauty consultant, and aesthetician. Years after my childhood, when I turned thirteen, the parental arguing began; that was not a happy time for anyone in our family. I hoped they would separate from one another for many nights so the unhappiness would end. Some nights, I wished I could turn up the radio's volume to make enough noise to drown the uncertainty of my parent's conversations. That was my first experience with anxiety and wondering what life would look like if we were no longer an intact family. I felt more disillusioned by marriage than I had ever imagined. My learned values and ethics became compromised and flushed down the toilet. I sometimes had no one to confide in that I thought could understand. I seemed very silent and lonely, wondering if I would experience the same one day in my marriage.

Soon after, it was my first year of college. My father eventually did leave our family home. I saw my mom grieving during the separation. I did not know how to help or if there could be any possible resolution. I traveled down that lonely road with my mom for about a year, listening to her worries about her marriage and our future. That was a sorrowful time that I wish could be erased from our minds. It is never easy as a young adult to navigate uncertainty regarding commitment in your own family home. It was often uneasy tension, and the environment was different as the level of peace and happiness was gone for a time. Happy memories seemed to become distorted as if they never happened.

It was very challenging for me to understand how a man could leave his family and martial oath to his heavenly Father for any circumstance or reason. Divorce was not what I was taught at home or in church. Our life as a family seemed like a lie after my family separated, and my life as a college student was upside down. I dropped courses that semester for various reasons, as I could not entirely focus. The feelings of insecurity and self-doubt came back. Profound sadness entered my life and kept a bookmark for me. The school had little meaning or excitement in my life. I would leave my classes, go to work, and come home to emptiness. The mixed messages about marriage and the reality of life made it hard for me to navigate my relationships on sound footing. Some of you may understand that your partner is one person at home but a different person in the workplace.

This type of living situation, a lack of genuine commitment, runs through many families, shaping and affecting each family member differently. Many kids begin experimenting with excessive drinking, drugs, suicidal thoughts, and self-harm, eventually ending in anger and rage.

Good parenting includes introducing our children to therapy. The goal would be to ease the pain of a commitment shattering while giving a new perspective to see their world differently through the guidance of a nonjudgmental and kind therapist.

The story of my early life has a beautiful ending, though. After some time, my father came back to our home. His return was good for an extended period. Later, another family dispute would play out, and my mother would remove herself from the house. Their history reveals that being separated does not necessarily encourage a permanent recommitment. I prayed for my parents for years during college, as I still do nightly. I was always hopeful my parents could find peace and a happier place in life; in time, they did find togetherness, and things seemed more promising. My parents are now in their late seventies and are still honoring their commitment together. For this, I am relieved they were a generation of strength and selflessness to overcome hard times. They chose to fight through their pains and differences to stay together. They broke the cycle of divorce which they had seen in other family members, and they instead embraced commitment!

Personal experience has taught me that our family dynamics, good and bad, affect not just ourselves but also our children's minds. I will always feel sad after going through those years of uncertainty in my family. It can create depression and anxiety for many, which does not disappear. I think there is a correlation between increased divorces and increased mental health issues. I see many patients who are divorced have significant anxiety and depression afterward. I see the similarities between children and adolescents of divorced parents. I've worked in mental hospitals for years, and the same issues would present themselves among patients repeatedly. Broken family's equal broken people. Our strengths can be like a superpower if we tap into them and use them positively.

These ideas make me think about the lies we tell ourselves to convince ourselves that divorce is a viable option, which was apparent in my marriage. Often divorce is driven by lust and selfishness. As intimacy decreases between married people, we must realize that date nights are necessary to keep us close to one another amid careers, children, and other obligations. Without date nights, couples may open a door and begin seeking attention from others. A pastor in Atlanta gives a particular sermon every year, telling a story about having his secretary drive in a separate car when they went to meetings. He then explained that it was best to have emails copied with another accountable person and not to have business meals alone with the opposite sex; meals can become intimate and are best served with your family.

I have always thought this wisdom to be brilliant because, as our culture changes, some may water this down and not believe it entirely. When relationships are compromised and having trouble, the temptation to commit adultery can be an easier trap to fall into. Maybe people cheat in relationships because they have little self-love and do not believe they are worthy of love. Instead, we could have a positive belief and be above reproach in our marriages and dating relationships. Practicing this helps close the gaps for complexity and pain to enter.

Secrets are the slow death of a relationship; they are temporary shields of hate. They never help or empower us and are not used to building solid foundations in a marriage. So, you may ask, why do we enhance the truth of our realities, avoid telling the whole truth, or convince ourselves that lies are better realities? Maybe it's because we are so broken and believe that it is better to stay in a marriage of status quo than face the truth of the unfortunate state of the union and decide to get a divorce. We are selfish with many desires, wanting what and when we want it. Our lives offer overwhelming choices, fed by TV and social media, not to be unhappy and always satisfied. Guess what? Life is going to have rough spots and unhappiness in it!

I still remember my marriage coach telling my husband, "If you choose to divorce, it will have a continued ripple effect over your entire family. It does not stop. There will be graduations, weddings, deaths, and more." To this, my husband stated, "I am getting out of here [the marriage]." I will never understand his response in the session, but I believe spiritual warfare is rich in deceiving many of us in our weak moments. However, I have chosen not to let this divorce be the end for me. I opened my eyes one day, picked myself up by the bootstraps, and began writing this book to heal myself and others.

The journey through divorce has been challenging for me; if you have children, it is even more challenging. And if you are going through a divorce, prepare yourself for waves of emotions but know you will make it out alive. There is no shortcut or go-pass ticket for you to buy. Your positive thinking and prayers can provide results for your future that you cannot gain without this experience. You will prevail by knowing yourself inside and out while walking through the desert and wilderness. So, what does commitment say about us? Does that say that we are secure, devoted, courageous, and forgiving of others as often as God asks?

Commitment is like slow-roasting nuts on a fire where you shouldn't rush it, or it will burn. It is vital to slow down to hear God's voice directing you. How can He not know what is best for our choices regarding commitment? He can grant you endurance and resilience, a true gift in a time of utter exhaustion.

Toolbox 2:

- A movie to add to the must-watch list for learning about honor and commitment: The Joy Luck Club 1993.
- Study True Commitment versus Uncommitted Vows equals dysfunctional living, divorce, and unforgivable pride.
- Dedication is loving your spouse even when you do not want to. It is having good self-control to choose responsibility over self-doubt (Genesis 4:7).
- Personal experience teaches and shapes family dynamics, both good and bad. It affects us and our children.
- We can break family destruction with new marital commitments.
- Our strengths can be like superpowers if we can tap into them and move positively, knowing our strengths and what we are capable of after enduring hard times.
- Secrets are the slow death of a relationship, and your emotional fortitude can prevail.
- Your positive thinking and prayers can provide results for your future that you cannot gain anywhere else.
- Endurance and resilience will get you through the steady haul.
- Do not allow yourself to be physically and

emotionally abused due to commitment. Abuse is never wanted. Study what God expects of us in marriage.

Chapter Three

What Is Domestication and Is It Real in Marriage?

Have you ever heard the word "domesticate" used as an adjective to describe ownership in a relationship? Maybe not, but you have generally understood the term used when talking about animals. Animals are either wild and feral or live indoors as domesticated pets. As a pet gains trust in their owner, they become more reliant.

I propose that a similar process occurs when some marriages and relationships become severely unbalanced as one loses leverage of respect for the other. One partner holds power over the other by taking more control in managing the marriage; this can make the other partner feel helpless and dependent in some regards and, therefore, domesticated, unable to do anything themselves. This example is more for marriages that are outside of truly godly marriages. Some people get to a point in their relationship where they feel they cannot live without the other person making most of the decisions. Instances like these are not a healthy management style in a relationship and can lead to resentment between spouses. In some ways, domestication is similar to codependence, where the person feels they must depend on the other to survive, especially in abusive relationships or marriages.

In some situations, domestication or dependence can be necessary in a marriage. For example, a person may be married to a disabled spouse who needs additional assistance in life, which is part of making a lifetime commitment to another person. It is hard to know what a marriage may encounter over the years. As marital partners age, there is no guarantee they both will stay healthy. Also, many unpredictable accidents happen throughout life, and one partner may need the other to make all or most of the decisions in life for the good of the marriage. There is also the subject of some religious cultures requiring the man to take over most decision-making. Keeping the various traditions in weddings can signify obedience and strong faith if it is part of being domesticated.

During therapy sessions throughout the years, I can recall many instances where clients, commonly female adults and older teens, felt an uncomfortable and unusual attachment to their spouse or partner. They did not describe this as love but more of a need to stay with someone for survival reasons because the partner or spouse was the leader. These individuals became addicted to unhealthy feelings, including dependency and incompetency, as their self-esteem plummeted, and they often felt trapped in the relationship. These clients eventually became more knowledgeable about receiving help and acknowledged that their behavior is based more on fear and unrealistic needs being met than love for the other person. Some individuals spoke about losing their ability to go out alone, balance a checkbook, pay monthly bills, and engage in self-care, which can lead to uncertainty in managing many areas of their lives.

Generally, this cycle begins with subtle control tactics by one partner, leading to increased and ongoing control by that individual in the relationship. After some years pass, couples can lose themselves so profoundly that many details of their existence and personalities start to diminish. Independence is no longer an option; eventually, they forget the value and importance of having responsibilities, independence, and freedom as individuals. Their self-confidence begins decreasing and can even disappear, a typical pattern of unhealthy domestication.

Relationships can slowly become unhealthy out of fear of one's ability to provide long-term care for themselves, which can then lead to personal shame and embarrassment. Some stay in a loveless marriage because of the level of guilt and determination for the relationship to continue instead of ending it. Those in this situation, both women and men, tend to be very young or in their middle to late stage of life (mid-fifties or older). They believe that it is harder to re-enter the business world or make a comfortable life for themselves than to end the relationship. The difficulty level in gaining suitable employment and sustaining a healthy independent lifestyle with low self-esteem during your senior years is almost impossible without your spouse's income. I say this with great truth from my experience and many others who have shared this topic.

Regrettably, women who experience a loss of independence and the ability to maintain a lifestyle to which they are accustomed can sink into deep depression. Fear can also be a culprit. It can paralyze your ability to think clearly. In my younger years of marriage, I made great money working in sales at Phillip Morris and later gained employment with G.D. Searle/Pfizer Pharmaceuticals. After a lifetime of hard work, I was led down a path to follow my dream or stay in the marriage I committed to. I chose the high road. After that monumental decision, I was never included, not once, in making any decisions on our livelihood, including discipline/corporal punishment. I never believed God intended me to have zero say in such decisions. Hearing him cry and call my name as his father spanked him wreaked my soul, but my former husband always locked the door, and I was never present, not once.

After my divorce, I could no longer break into the pharmaceutical sales industry, where I made good money, had excellent health insurance, and had a 401(k)savings plan. All the perks and security were gone. It made me feel fearful, anxious, and sad for many days. I still had to depend on my former husband to supply an option from work to have my health insurance continue. This dependence came at a substantial financial expense and keeping that option for a short year was a battle. A few months later, I felt like a homeless person shopping for any health insurance I could afford after having a premium policy for twenty-one years of marriage.

I realized that all I had done in the marriage was to help my husband gain his successful employment and have a wedge drawn between me and my precious son. Now, the company I sacrificed countless hours of work for—writing payroll checks, balancing the books, and running as an errand girl—was worth nothing to me but everything to him. He had his successful business, money to do as he pleased, and a new life. His success would all be wonderful if this story was about a single man without a wife and child or an honest stake that he shared.

You have heard of friends or neighbors with similar sad stories. There are truthful and heart-breaking stories of many women without health insurance and who cannot afford it. I believe that many selfish and careless people do this intentionally to their unwanted spouses, just abandoning them and feeling justified for doing it. This behavior is unbiblical. We must remember that domestication has excellent power, just as in choosing to divorce your spouse.

I was in my mid-fifties at the time of the divorce. I felt used, like a piece of trash left behind. My options were minimal due to my age to move on. It affected the availability of my future in healthcare, careers, and financial stabilization.

There are many types of psychological issues that many of us face. The toll of domestication has brought some women, especially mothers, to self-harming and suicidal behaviors. The rising number of depressive women is astounding; research women and depression or women in mental facilities. I remember when I thought I was going to be homeless. My health insurance (Cobra) lapsed by no fault of mine, and I could not get any assistance from my former husband, from whom the policy originated. I was hospitalized at Emory a year and a half after my divorce. That one night in the trauma unit at Emory was over $20,000. It made me realize that compassion for other women in similar circumstances is necessary.

Leaving a relationship that has tremendous power over you is never easy. I began working three jobs after the divorce to maintain a better lifestyle. One of the jobs was in the emergency room, where I was a trauma assessment specialist. My shift was sometimes being called out in the middle of the night to talk to the families of dying or deceased individuals after a suicide attempt or completion. I was privy to hearing many stories, many including break-ups and divorces. I remember spending hours talking to women barely holding on to life, with rope burns around their necks in failed attempts to take their own lives due to facing love loss and failed relationships. There are examples of domestication that need to stop destroying the minds of others, making them think they can't survive without their marriage. The suicide rate for divorced adults is three times that of married adults, as the Centers for Disease Control's annual Multiple Cause of Death Files report reveals.

These experiences made me focus on my loss in my marriage. I remember lying awake so many nights, wondering how dependent I became on my marriage. I was highly educated and made six figures before marrying at thirty. Before tying the knot, I was excited and happy about life and had enough money and a great future to live comfortably. I had no pressing reasons to marry when I did, except for true love. My relationship with Christ was good, and I had been praying and fasting with a friend for my husband to be an honorable and Godly man. Eventually, I thought I was making one of the best decisions of my life, choosing a husband and becoming a wife, later, a stay-at-home mom and less of a career woman.

Marriage was a personal and spiritual goal I had always believed would be fantastic with the right person. It could be successful or equally dangerous without a good and faithful choice. Since I had waited to get married in my thirties, I believed I had enough discernment to make a wise mate choice. God had brought my "perfect" mate after years of dating others. I remember that he was handsome, innovative, and, above all, a professing Christian. He seemed to know his Bible well, and we shared many of the same beliefs. We attended church together and seemed to have many common morals and values. It all seemed so perfect to me.

I paid close attention to my future husband's family and their interaction. Everything seemed to check out mainly, as they seemed normal enough. It seemed odd that the exterior was so average like the old TV show *Leave It to Beaver*. Little did I know the substantial role my facade played in the introduction of my domestication and how it would later impact the decline of our marriage.

My former husband and I were both firstborn and had Type A personalities; that should have been enough for me to realize that conflicts would readily arise. We both wanted to be right in many situations, which brought on various arguments unless I was willing to be submissive and let it go. I can remember rarely being apologized to, no matter how much it hurt. I believe that personality types can influence the direction of domestication in a relationship with damaging communication from the start. If one person is a high extrovert and the other is more of an introvert with increased feelings, domestication has the perfect breeding ground to emerge.

Regarding personality types, for example, based on the Myers-Briggs personality test, the Extravert-Intuitive-Thinker–Judger (ENTJ) personality type is stated to be naturally assertive and decisive. This personality type has more characteristics that can dominate and control a relationship. The ENTJs generally don't naturally handle their emotions well and seem noteworthy in insensitivity to others unless there is a personal motive. This group of people rarely understand or care how their significant others feel. They seem to be more interested in themselves. A good and statistically savvy test can help discover if a couple should advance in marriage. A clever quote by Don Marquis is, "Ideas pull the trigger, but instinct loads the gun."

There were a few more things in life that I wish my parents had taught me growing up. Maybe better instincts and how to sharpen them. Godly relationship experiences are imperative while you are young, as well as while you are dating. They promote a healthy environment and platform for an honest relationship that grows in a marriage. In hindsight, I wish there had been a class or retreat to teach couples how to resolve conflict and actual, genuine forgiveness before the wedding. I never recognized many of the red flags to look for in a relationship. I am convinced this may have helped avoid some vicious cycles of bad relationships that many know well, preventing us from going from one unhealthy relationship to another.

I want others to learn from this book that you can be an excellent and healthy decision-maker during dating and marriage. Look for ways to have you and your significant other take classes together and make sure you are a good fit before the wedding, personality-wise. Before marriage, learn what you like and do not like about each other. Understand how much compromise and compassion it takes for a continuous, joyful union. Think about introducing children to the marriage and how you will raise them while ensuring the marriage is stable and healthy enough for the added stress. Some people may not be cut out to be compatible partners or parents, especially when under the influence of domestication.

I grew up in a very traditional home, and my parents were an upper-middle-class family. I watched how my father was always motivated to provide for my mother and me before my younger brother was born. For the most part, in my parents' generation, the man paid all or most of the living expenses. The woman would leave her parents' home, and the new responsibility of caring for her was transferred to her new husband in marriage. When I left to get married, I thought it only natural for my husband to care for me. Going to dinners, theaters, and many excursions felt good while my husband paid the way for us. It was a nice feeling of security and devotion. I counted on him to eventually take over our finances and future planning of our lives after the wedding.

Unfortunately, who knew that one day in my future, this man who did all this so-called caring for me would end our marriage by serving me divorce papers? Who knew that the electric company would knock on my door in the middle of winter while my elderly babysitter cared for our young, sick son and turned off the power while still married? Who knew football games and long weekends with the boys would be more important than staying home with our family? I was just a new mother and had no training in caring for a child, just off-life support. Suppose I can help a handful of people through this book by pointing out things to be aware of before getting married to steer the person to a better destination instead of unhealthy domestication in marriage. In that case, it will be worth sharing my journey.

If we make a list today of what we may want in a partner and, more importantly, what we do not wish to do and stick to it, there will be better odds that things will work in our favor. Taking a personality test, as a start, might improve your odds of avoiding becoming domesticated and trapped in a marriage you don't want. It is time to see through more transparent glasses than rose-colored ones. For instance, I made a list shortly *after* I divorced what I would be delighted to find in a man in his fifties. Here is my list of my top twenty desired characteristics:

1. A man after God's heart (prays with his wife and family).
2. A man of honor (goes without defining).
3. A man filled with courage (can be a mentor to others struggling in marriage).
4. A man of integrity (does not put himself in vulnerable situations).
5. A man of faithfulness (asks for help and accountability before being tempted to cheat).
6. A man of gratefulness (embraces the differences between a man and woman).
7. A financially responsible man (does not ignore God's plan of responsibility).
8. A man of laughter (not at his wife but with her).
9. A man of extraordinary listening abilities (attentive and mindful of his listening skills).
10. A man of vulnerability (honesty and morality).

11. A man without pride (putting his family first).
12. A humble man (not just in front of others).
13. A generous man (not just for their benefit).
14. A man with a transparent and loving heart (without secrets and lies).
15. A man with a robust and compassionate heart (who puts others needs above himself).
16. A man of balanced sensitivity (who does not ignore when his partner is in pain).
17. A physically strong man (who does not sleep and leaves most weekends).
18. A man who thinks outside the box and enjoys resolving issues instead of hiding them.
19. He is an exciting man who has a work life balance.
20. A man who delights in wandering and traveling together exploring.
21. A man who applauds a woman of independence.

I consider having a list of things you cannot compromise on equally important. Moreover, they are your deal-breakers in a relationship. One could spare many tears if a person could see the incompatibility before commitment. My deal-breakers are easy:

- Breaking God's commandments without remorse
- A history of continuous lying
- Stealing another's wife
- Full-blown pridefulness

Although life can be filled with all kinds of disappointment, it is possible to foresee some events of strategic control occurring in a relationship, as the idea of getting comfortable with who you are, who you have chosen, and following God is more important. In retrospect, I could spend a lifetime trying to dissect my failed marriage, but I was not blind to the gradual decline and loss of my authentic self and a marriage not working anymore. However, I decided not to beat myself up about choices and instead learn from the relational devastation.

Perhaps some of us allow others to control us to feel loved. Many are trapped with few ideas of resolving things, but fear-domestication drives us to stay in unhealthy relationships because we think it is love. Generally, good or bad relationships do not accept change well, as we want the status quo to remain the same. Ultimately, trying to steer any relationship in a new direction becomes difficult. In my relationship, we reached a point where there was a path of no return. I know that many clients shared similar stories with me about their struggles, and it is hard to believe another human being could have done these monstrous acts toward their once beloved bride or groom.

I never knew the word "contentious" until my divorce. Contentious is a negative word that describes a self-centered person who has lost the ability to open their heart. As I learned more about the many traits of a contentious person, I decided it was no longer suitable for me, mentally or physically, to remain inside the marriage. I understand how to be a more productive Christian and protect myself from further attacks.

I grew physically sick knowing I fell for someone like this, married them and had a child. This life became impossible with all the unsolvable demands during our marriage.

Toolbox 3:

- Domestication can create an addiction to unhealthy feelings, including dependency and incompetency. Your self-worth and self-esteem begin to plummet.
- Relationships can slowly become unhealthy out of fear of one's ability to care for oneself as a form of domestication slowly enters your life.
- Do not allow your children to be subject to a life of manipulation and domestication. They cannot grow up to be efficient and independent if their role model barely survives.
- Be in prayer and be aware!
- Know that instincts are born but can be sharpened to help eliminate potentially harmful relationships.
- Look for red flags of controlling behaviors before marriage.
- Your spouse may be enabling you on purpose.
- Be willing to take pre-marital tests with a therapist specializing in weddings or with a psychologist.
- Do not enter into a relationship until you have enough self-love and self-respect.
- Do not believe you cannot care for yourself or that no one else will love you. These are lies that a controller will try to convince you.
- Seek pastoral care when you feel you cannot leave your marriage.

Chapter Four

How Real Is Narcissism and Gaslighting?

I have come to learn what it is like to face the monster, devoid of low or dimensive empathy. Most people have heard of narcissism, where an individual who is cruel and deliberately gains control of another person for their agendas. Understand that some individuals can be disloyal and have a nature to suppress their humanity. They can be very contentious and hard to live with. Their behaviors are only purposeful, and some with more malice than others. They generally exhibit a disregard for other people's feelings. The intent is to strip away another person's identity who is in love to gain more attention and control, making for an unequal relationship balance. The leverage gets lost on one's behalf. The decision-making becomes difficult, and the love we once imagined is often only disgusting to one another. Most friends and family notice the sick behavior way before the individual in the relationship can see the trickery happening to them.

Narcissists are great at their game, and it seems to come naturally. They hinder the other person's ability to believe they can function independently and gradually steal their confidence. Then, they make sure the person believes that they need them in their life to continue living, which might be how domestication begins in many relationships. It is a vicious web that the spider tries to catch you in. Later, you become entangled in the web, and it can take years before you can truly see it happening so that you can escape. This trap is a debilitating lifestyle for most.

Narcissists are generally good at push-and-pull relational behavior, somewhat like a tug-of-war game. It's almost like I want you, and 5 minutes later, I don't want you. You can seamlessly feel like the crazy one and have a sense of solid power in the relationship. These feelings are neither expected nor healthy behavior. If you stay long enough, there are psychological pitfalls that you will most likely experience and happiness that you will never find. Many narcissists are never diagnosed with this dangerous personality disorder. I only had one couple in 8 years ask for help. Honestly, how many narcissists do you think line up for mental use? Some people have narcissistic tendencies but do not fit the DSM5 diagnosis, which is a scary thought.

In my relationship, I left my family and a beautiful life near Virginia Beach when I got married. I had lived in Virginia for many years and made great friendships while there, but I did not know anyone in Georgia, where I moved to pursue what seemed to be love. My boyfriend at the time, later husband, had a large family and extended large family, all within a hundred miles of him, so I thought I was gaining an awesome family after leaving mine. Honestly, who could not be excited to move for a new beginning, for love, marriage, and a new life?

But my life unraveled quickly, as there was obvious trouble for us after the first year of marriage. He questioned my prior Catholic faith and my maturity level in Christianity. Just months after marriage, the lack of intimacy began the downfall of our relationship. It is hard to swallow as a wife when someone you love enjoys looking in magazines of seductive women posing for the annual *Sports Illustrated Swimsuit Edition*. While some may think that is silly, I thought these models in the magazine were very sensual like soft porn. I believe this is how many relationships begin the downfall of intimacy in a marriage. I am unsure how long this had been going on, but other things did not increase my trust in or love for my husband. I paid the bills in the first part of my marriage when my husband started his career. When the cable bills came in the mail and included pornographic movie titles that I had never purchased or watched, I became concerned. I was so upset by these charges that I remember calling the cable company and making a fool of myself, trying to dispute what could not be denied. I could not understand while my son and I traveled to visit my family after my father had serious surgery, and the exact dates appeared on the cable bill for these movies. Besides the distastefulness of feeling betrayed, there was the struggle with reaching standards that no longer existed in our marriage. I will allow you to judge if this happened or if it was a mere mistake on our cable bill. That said, why do some men need to have trash in their lives when they are married?

The truth of marriage was diminishing daily, but he always appeared generous and wore a phony smile even minutes after arguing with me in front of my son and leaving me in the car just minutes before church. Few in that church knew our truth, but some suspected it and later spoke with me about the battles in a small church to take sides in other unstable marriages. When seductive women enter a married man's mind, nothing good can come from it, whether in a book, magazine, or person. I was told I could continue attending church, but my husband wanted to bring a new friend (woman) to church. His arrogance was troubling, and

I started to participate less and less. I reached the point where I no longer cared who wanted to accompany him.

My self-esteem plummeted during my marriage, and I felt insecure. I realized I depended on someone, no longer a man I could trust. However, I was fearful about leaving our marriage but could not tell you why, other than feeling like a failure and no one would ever love me again because my divorce broke me. When one person holds all the keys to your lifeline, you become, by nature, helpless. Doing so is never a good situation for anyone, man or woman. A predator would probably eat you if you were an animal in the forest.

Another example of this twisted living is remembering specific conversations. I had spoken of adoption many times before marriage and during the marriage. Later, he acted as if the topic of adoption was a foreign conversation that had never taken place between us. There were applications that my dear aunt had helped me complete. Also, there were many phone calls to adoption agencies, even in Ukraine, but my husband never expressed any interest in following up, even on just one. Life no longer seemed normal or safe for me. I will never know if he was a true narcissist, but I lived in a relationship I would never enter again in my now wiser future.

What are the signs of Gaslighting?

Fast-forward to staying in the marriage, ten years later, I became pregnant and unfortunately was faced with the saddest news a mother could handle. I went to my doctor's office at 6:00 a.m. on Monday and waited in the hall alone until the office opened at 8:00 a.m. It was one of the most tearful times of my entire life. I was very sick (not knowing I was pregnant), and my husband had gone to a Christmas party the evening before and was very angry because I did not attend, so I went to the doctor alone that morning. I tried to explain that I felt ill and could not make it. There was no justification I could construct for him to realize that I could not attend a big party. That morning, I discovered one of the biggest blessings a woman can experience. I was pregnant! My husband's pride and stubbornness allowed him to lay in bed and stay with a defeatist attitude while I drove myself throwing up to the doctor thirty minutes away. Hours later, I was alone when the doctor confirmed my suspicion of pregnancy with the only child we would ever have together.

After talking to many wise friends, I am convinced that many women can be the perfect victims of narcissistic victimization. Gas lighting is another part of the game. It is a recognizable pattern and will make you believe every wrong incident is your fault. I continued explaining my fatigue, nausea, and inability to attend his work party, but he would not hear of it. At that moment, I knew I was not alone in my marriage but alone in life to raise a child. I was in shock and could not process the loveless marriage I had to live in. That morning, the doctor confirmed my pregnancy had progressed to the end of the first trimester despite no previous signs of pregnancy. When the technician did the ultrasound, it showed two babies—a set of twins. My doctor had known me for 10 years. I shared with him the ups and downs. I could see the sadness in his eyes as he delivered the news to me alone. I sat with him inconsolable in the office for a few hours, trying to decide how to get through this. My marriage changed from what I anticipated, especially regarding raising a Godly child.

After my doctor called my house numerous times, and I had texted with no response, my husband eventually arrived at the doctor's office several hours later. I had already gone downstairs and had an emergency ultrasound. Then, they escorted me into a small room with a geneticist, a social worker, and another particular doctor. They strongly encouraged me not to proceed with the pregnancy due to many severe birth deformities and other abnormalities identified after the ultrasound and amniocentesis. My head spun so fast it seemed like I entered another nightmare. There was my terrible marriage and now more complicated life and death issues. The decision to continue the pregnancy became easy for me, as I have always believed that children are gifts of God. I knew one solid truth: God knows best for me and would never leave me. I wanted his will to be done and trusted him more than anyone.

As the emotional support began dwindling, my husband also became physically unavailable. The distant behavior was increasing month by month. I felt pressure to decide to keep my baby and prayed for God's wisdom and protection daily. My husband did not pray with me and continued business as usual (late nights, business dinners, challenging to reach by phone calls or texting). If I knew the true nature of my marriage, my loyalty would have never been given to him. I had to be blind to those things and focus on keeping a child alive.

Shortly after, the second ultrasound showed only one fetus made it; a travesty to hear. I distinctly remember that my husband had an urgent call at the office he needed to attend to, and I began to see the struggles with my pregnancy would be a situation that I needed to handle by myself. I understood I would have to get stronger and gain Godly support to manage the marriage and high-risk pregnancy. The void was hard to accept, and the lack of joy and marital love did not surround our first child's birth. I was now entering a new life of great responsibility to care for a child with many life-threatening medical illnesses. My emotions about the failing marriage needed to be on the back burner as I focused on all the changes to keep my son alive and healthy.

I think God granted me a chance for a change and brought a breath of life back into my world. Nothing was too big for God, but nothing about this situation made sense. In having this child, I hoped to regain my independence. I moved to Gainesville, Florida, and lived in a small apartment for five weeks before surgery. I resided close to the hospital to travel back and forth. My husband never stopped working, and I slept alone for many nights with thousands of thoughts running through my mind. How could someone as insightful as myself not see that I was wrong about this man I loved?

The incredible surgeon and all the nurses made it worth it. I remember sending them cards to let them know how gracious they were for all they did in their lives. We continued to follow up with the surgeon for many years for checkups and visited the nurses on the unit. We used to try to find our unique ceiling tile from the room, which my mother and father helped draw while we spent hours at the hospital. It was art therapy for all of us.

Once we returned to Atlanta after about four months, I fell asleep on the sofa with my little bundle of joy many nights. Our lives have changed significantly. There were so many doctor appointments that I lost count. The safety net that Romeo, my son, required was high. He could not have contact with many people in the first few years due to life-threatening germs. I tried to preserve his immune system constantly. He had one fully developed lung, and the other one was compromised. His heart and lungs had to share space with his stomach, kidney, liver, and other vital organs. There was a handmade gortex patch as big as the bottom of a Pepsi can that was placed inside him to keep those organs lowered. He experienced a feeding tube and several surgeries.

We ended up spending a lot of the time alone. Everything was as usual for my husband: going into the office, having team-building dinners with the office staff, and entertaining clients. His clients became increasingly important to him after he changed jobs and began his own company. My thoughts of having a deeply committed Christian family were fading quickly. Many evenings, Romeo and I sat home alone while my husband missed dinners and valuable time as he spent increasing time with his co-workers; the new routine was team-building.

    I never once put a job or co-worker before my child or husband. I believe that this is asking for comprising situations for a family. Romeo and I had fun as he began to travel, making new friends as he got older. He received a costly shot each year for his lung protection, which allowed us to increase where he could go. We joined mom groups with home-schooled children. Romeo developed friendships and social times with other children. As the years went on, Romeo asked for a sibling. I knew it would never happen. My husband had shifted to work fulfillment, and the imbalance changed our marriage forever. I became increasingly focused on my child and less on worrying about gaslighting and game-playing. I ended up with zero tolerance for that nonsense. I believe a shift in thinking slowly led us down a path until our divorce. Thankfully, everything has a silver lining, and I am grateful, looking back, that I had a chance to be married and have a fantastic son.

Toolbox 4:

- When one partner holds all power over the other by taking more control in the management and decision-making of the marriage, domestication has begun. Thus, selfish behavior can develop.
- Get to know your boundaries what you are willing to accept and will not. Learn your deal-breakers so that you never become a victim of narcissism.
- Know what a manipulating relationship looks like, for a narcissist can ruin your life.
- Read and research gas lighting. If you are gas-lit into believing you are crazy, get a professional opinion to know the truth and prepare a new and healthy life for yourself and your children.
- Be careful of the tug-of-war game; this is a red flag.
- Look for the shift in power in your relationship.
- Never look back. If you were married, some goodness would come from that, such as children. (Remember the silver lining; everything has a silver lining.)
- Join a group specifically for understanding narcissism and gaslighting behaviors.

Chapter Five

A Life Can Be Made Shameless

How did the thought of leaving someone whom you had promised eternity with, inversely, become such a desensitized and matter-of-fact topic in life? Has society plummeted so far in morality that we view commitment as unnecessary, unattractive, and disposable? Are character and integrity no longer valued attributes in humanity? Sadly, I think answering these questions is complicated but ultimately will bring an individual closer to truth and closure in life. Many events today are considered to be accepted by some in society but are healthy for a Christian marriage. What level of shame are we willing to ignore or take?

Does finding an end to an awful marriage give us some level of closure, shame, or relief? It is hard enough to make our own bad decisions, but living with someone else's decision to leave you is never easy or forgotten. Our culture today seems to be shaming us for staying in bad marriages and views divorce as more of a relief and wise choice. Many want to be happy or happier, leaving a wedding for a better opportunity. Why do we constantly think we must focus on "the desire to be happier?" I wonder that when I hear people say, "God wants us to be happy." In retrospect, I understand what they are trying to convey, but the Bible says there will be suffering and consequences in life, and due to our sinful natures, we will not always be happy.

Following through on ending a relationship can seem like just another business transaction at the end of the day. It's a relief and a solution for some people. Maybe spouses feel they did not get what was due to them, or there is a much more enticing person luring them away and encouraging the divorce. In the following text, I hope to make a clear case and unwind some people's soulless and shaming behaviors during a divorce, whether they are staying or leaving a marriage. We are beings of poor judgment sometimes. I wish we could forgive freely.

My story began one day in college, where my most pivotal experience would unfold; I would remember what was to come for many years. It could have changed my faith and altered my belief in a truly committed relationship with God. An economics professor mentioned that relationships mimic the supply and demand curve. When the connection is good, the supply of what each person needs in the relationship is met. On the contrary, when the connection is unhealthy, the demands are unmet. This concept made me wonder if some people feel they deserve more just because they are unhappy in their marriages. I wish I knew why "Deserving and being privileged to abundant happiness" is the highlight of importance in any relationship, especially in marriage. This type of selfishness seems to be increasing over the generations. Every decade, I watch the selfish movement become furious, as those who can imagine choosing to roll up a relationship neatly like a paper airplane and sail it off to the bottom of the sea do so, in with the new and out with the out. There will always be those who discard genuine humanity and committed relationships for something else, which is highly concerning!

Many will be blinded by the illusions of a promising new business, enticing new and younger partners to marry, switching gender experiences, or simply the desire to have freedom again as reasons for a divorce. I worry about their integrity and commitment to God first, then to their children left behind without a committed parental unit of a mother and father. Here is how shame can enter our lives and start chipping away at what God intended for us—a life of hope, not guilt.

It is worth wondering what goes through a person's mind as they rationalize their choices. These alterations, which they are fully aware of, will change their lives forever. Many divorces cause permanent, irrefutable damage to our souls and grieving hearts, and no one can put a time limit on healing a broken heart and the fear associated with the deep-seated shame of a failed marriage. It can take years of therapy to decrease the depression, guilt, and anxiety over the breakup. Some people have escalated mental illness, resulting in diagnoses of post-traumatic stress disorder (PTSD) from the horrific battle of the mind as they try to normalize the experience of a divorce.

Mental illness can be triggered and amplified at times of trauma; I have seen it happen many times. The one leaving the marriage doesn't want to take on any responsibility or negativity that can be associated with a spouse's increased mental illness through a divorce. I have heard the words ring in my marriage, "You're crazy!" This emotional twist of words can take on many faces afflicted more by mental illness and is one of many other shaming behaviors. Little positivity is left after your mind convinces you of all the shame in your life. It diminishes hope. I know many clients whose lives became messes with alcohol and drugs because they could not handle their new addiction coping skills. Due to this challenging personal situation, some lost their children during the divorce. Hearing the stories of women who had never had any mental illness before but, years after divorce, still struggle with addiction to prescription drugs or alcohol to cope with mental issues crushed my heart. Their stories are due to unbearable stress and false truths (shame) that some must live within their marriages for years until they divorce. My former husband often accused me of twisting and blurring facts until the truth prevailed.

If only more husbands felt remorse for what they allow their left-behind partners to go through. I will see the ever-ingrained smirk on my former husband's face as he crushed all my ideas of the hopeful future. Husbands can be spiteful and devious, as we all can be without a nurtured heart and God-fearing faith. Each husband and wife have a choice. Nevertheless, many husbands make their wives feel as if she is the one who is crazy and unstable, destroying the image that God gave them. I think some husbands can gain some false sense of euphoria instead of shame for divorces. I feel confident this also happens with women doing this to their husbands. Whatever faith a person comes from, for marriage at its end, there should be a sense of honorable treatment toward one another. An ex-wife is still the mother of the children; without respect and regard for her, how will a child grow up to be respectful and loving in a relationship, all while with a confusion of love in their hearts for each parent?

Instead, men and women can make their spouses destroy every thread of their once-happy lives together by making them feel worthless and hated. For example, in front of my son, my former husband was demanding by acting like I was stupid and that my achievements in college and work weren't exceptional. My son was not allowed to stay at my home during high school exams and other times because my former husband made my son feel I was incapable of helping him with projects or tests. There were other times when I had made CAT scans or MRI appointments for my son, and my husband would arrive early to tell the staff our son needed to go back with only him. All while I was still picking him up from school, feeding him, and driving to those appointments. At twelve, my son lost respect for me from this constant bantering with my husband. In those times, I tried to recall this verse over and over, "That is why, for Christ's sake, I delight in weaknesses, insults, hardships, persecutions, difficulties. For when I am weak, then I am strong" (2 Corinthians12:10).

Divorce is the product of so many illusions of a life that stem from dissatisfaction at that moment for one or both spouses and the simple greed of thinking we deserve more. Divorce thinking can be very spontaneous and impulsive. People who strive for constant excitement can easily fear boredom, taking people down many disrespectful paths, such as a lack of fidelity. In this case, many of us are trying to recover from the truth that our beloved spouse has decided to forget and destroy our vows. They begin living two lives; I call this a twisted dual life with a selfish desire constantly to be stimulated. It is a lack of self-control and self-respect. These irrational, unfaithful behaviors are simply examples of increased self-centeredness and a lack of regard for the commitment once promised to one another. At least for Christians, this promise and covenant we made with God in His house and in front of His people who were asked, "Will you promise to uphold this marriage and help these two people be accountable for their marriage?"

I wonder if parents understand that putting a child first during a high-conflict divorce is the right thing to do instead of all their needs. There needs to be a balance, and therapists specialize in this type of counseling. Many things happen quickly and without good counsel. Never feel pressured to sign documents and make quick decisions during divorce because that is when you need great prayer and wise counsel to assist in long and short-term decisions for the best possible results.

I still wonder, five years later, if I made all the right decisions. I did my homework, networked with specific people in the field, and tried my best with the motivation I could manage. I was never allowed to contact my former husband's family after the divorce. That was very difficult after twenty-two years of sharing holidays, heartaches, and other family events with them. I never heard once from his family, and it was as if I wore a scarlet letter on my back. It was like they had signed a contract, which they did not, so why the silence?

I wonder if people committing the affairs ever step out of their fantasy world to acknowledge what the effects of the matter will have on their children once they are in relationships as teens or adults. I counsel teens and college-aged students, and they often reveal their parents' affairs many years later, affecting them and keeping the grueling pain inside of them. They are generally angry and have acted out toward others in one form or another. They struggle with the details they may have learned about their father or mother or finally have enough maturity to figure out all the lies and secrets they told them. What a mess!

While many are unmarried, many teens and college-aged students have repeated the same secretive behavior in their romantic relationships with girlfriends and boyfriends. They sit in shame and need genuine guidance and help to move forward from their parent's divorce. Is it not sad that some parents are sending and teaching our young-minded children this sick and characterless morality?

Shameful behaviors do not end there. Today, it is common to

have divorce parties to celebrate the loss and end of life with a spouse. I am not saying in some marriages, it is a relief for it to be over. Is this the message and role model we want to send as the mother of our children? I remember hearing this often in my home, "Do what you want and ask for forgiveness later." Is there nothing more acceptable or constructive to reflect on our children? I think our society has sometimes become immune to letting go of whatever does not feel good in exchange for finding a quick replacement or temporary happiness, encouraging this shameful behavior. I cannot get comfortable with the term, "This is the new normal and, just like a steamroller, move on."

Where are the feelings of disgrace and dishonor when an adult leaves a committed marriage? It seems there is little remorse, believing, "In with the new and out with the old." Here is one of my favorite quotes by the late Joseph B. Wirthlin I found during my divorce that seems to ring true, "How the beautiful things around us become invisible to us because we take them for granted."

I still remember feeling like I was easily replaceable as his wife. He must work later, skip family dinners, and dismiss my phone calls. As a mother, I felt embarrassed by what was happening to myself and my son. While some may have thought being a wife was tremendous and esteemed, I knew it was dissectible by others. I found it challenging to try and teach my son Christian attributes of integrity and the importance of commitment as he was a teen because of what was happening around him; some children are already so predisposed to be self-centered at that age. I was challenged by many biblical issues concerning my husband that I had never dreamed of, and I had to always be on guard to explain a different version of things to my son that once was believed.

A good example was drinking. My former husband seemed to misuse scripture to justify his sinful behavior by teaching my son it was okay to drink wine because Jesus did it. However, he left out the most crucial element of this Bible story: He drank the fresh wine He created. As a result, my former husband often conveyed a late night with fellow workers drinking as acceptable. There is a great verse that sums up why this behavior is not acceptable.

Isaiah 5:20 states, "Woe to those who call evil good and good evil, who put darkness for light and light for darkness, who put bitter for sweet and sweet for bitter!"

We should never make a person feel ashamed for their actions or beliefs. This behavior opens doors to remorseful actions. I wanted a happier ending in my marriage and sought every avenue I knew to fix the drowning I constantly felt, from morning until night. As time passed, he felt better educated than me and was uninterested in my thoughts or opinions. He began going against most things that I had taught my son. As I look back, I feel convinced of 1 Corinthians 15:33 happening in my marriage, "Do not be deceived: 'Bad company ruins good morals.'" A family man coming home excited to have dinner and pray with his family was only a distant dream for my marriage.

Shame can also come from believing in the transparency of your spouse as they go off to work. You might expect the same person to come home at the end of the day. However, I saw something entirely different in my marriage. There were so many days that I could not quite grasp the magnitude of the daily changes happening to my husband; it was like a stranger entering my home. I could not overcome the cleverness and constant feeling that something was happening without proof. Finally, I spent my weekly salary on a private investigator for peace of mind. We eventually decided to use a tracker put on my husband's car. The investigator called me daily to explain what events happened during the day. Finally, my husband found the tracker and had it removed on a day of travel. It was good that I had a backup person watching for this to happen. We knew when he detached it; therefore, the investigator could still do his job, but it was just more costly to me because he crushed the tracker into pieces.

All people of faith suffer when dishonesty becomes visible in a marriage or life. Some believe it is improper or disrespectful to discuss the unhappiness in a marriage, except in a closed room with a marital therapist. Other individuals may live in silent agony due to their culture not allowing or believing in an intervention for a marriage, such as therapy. I commend those who can seek support and begin understanding the value of counseling and a journey to heal during and after divorce. The varying, duplicitous events outside the marriage are sometimes never brought to light or spoken of.

As a therapist, I thought it best to begin seeking counseling when divorce was considered an option in our home. Counseling was one of the best resources that led me to see the truth, hence becoming closer to God during the years of personal suffering. While I could not afford outlets other than my Christian marriage counselor, it is good to know that a Christian group called Divorce Recovery exists. This program is a free, 12-week group that many organizations offer at churches to help with feelings of shame and hurt during or after the divorce. The support was beneficial, and the people I met on that journey were irreplaceable. I remember feeling restored, little by little, each week while attending the group.

I learned that families can choose to turn a blind eye to what is happening in a marriage and be ill-equipped to help their children through divorce. If we rely only on family, then sometimes the fictional truths in marriage continue until the removal of the facade reveals hidden issues. I always wanted a healthy relationship based on a united and honorable commitment, but we don't always get what we want. We marry in a church, synagogue, or other precious place, repeating sacred vows to our life partners, guests, and higher power. Do we promise the union of our souls, or has the ceremony become a formality in today's society? Do we look toward keeping ourselves sacred and reaching out for wholesome mentors to assist us through hard times? How likely is it that we have persons who help us keep our spoken commitment through being accountable?

I grew up for many years as a Catholic, and it was drilled into our brains to dismiss feelings of attraction to others in a committed relationship, have good self-control that leads to good character, and avoid situations where you could be vulnerable to adultery. I did not learn until my teens about the secret world of infidelity in relationships. It seemed so dark and wicked that people would sneak around on their boyfriends/girlfriends and husbands/wives.

From experience, we are permanently different after we suffer the death of a relationship: the terrain shifts and changes to a new life of being single. We cannot go back and often wonder if we will ever fit in again as we watch our married friends continue their marital journeys. The "new normal" is what we are left to embrace. Separating from someone you committed your whole life to will never feel normal.

The suffering and shameful feelings from a marriage that ends seem like they go on for a lifetime. Here is one of my favorite verses, as it helps me calm this feeling when it brings me down: "Not only so, but we also glory in our sufferings, because we know that *suffering produces perseverance*; perseverance, character; and character, hope" (Romans 5:3-5).

Toolbox 5:

- Shame can form when leaving a marriage or staying in a destructive one.
- Many divorces cause permanent, irrefutable damage and grieving hearts, but you can still get extra help from free divorce recovery groups. They can help encourage balance when a marital covenant breaks and how to grow from it.
- Never forget that, in most instances, "bad company ruins good morals."
- Beware when changes begin to occur. Never be too busy for your marriage. Make your commitment solid.
- No one can put a time limit on healing a broken heart and the fear associated with the deep-seated shame of a failed marriage. Take your time to heal.
- Isaiah 5:20 states, "Woe to those who call evil good and good evil, who put darkness for light and light for darkness, who put bitter for sweet and sweet for bitter!"
- It can take years of therapy to decrease the depression, shame, and anxiety over the breakup. Never give up!

Chapter Six

Society and It's Darkness

In therapy, I see many divorced and divorcing clients stricken with darkness, shame, depression, heightened anxiety, and so much more. They all have one thing in common: fear and the low probability of defending themselves properly from the dark footprint of divorce. There seems to be no shield or fairness during this dark war that leads to the finality of divorce for a marriage. I wish we could invent something to protect against the torment, lies, and deceit that some divorce often unleashes. Such an incredible product with superpowers for protection could make millions (only in a sci-fi movie). Just think what would happen if an alarm went off on our phones when our spouses think of committing acts contradictory to a committed marriage.

While not all divorces end due to breaking a wedding vow, many behavioral economists believe we make bad choices when hungry, which means that when we desire something and open the door to it, we get drained by that choice. It is as simple as going to the grocery store when hungry. We tend to buy way more than we need and get tempted by so many choices that we tend to gorge. This idea can be related to lowered inhibitions when a married person grows tempted to go places married people should not go. It only leads to immediate disaster or a festering desire to go back. What you want now may not be what you want the most. Much of our destruction correlates with your decision of what you want. Paul, the apostle, spoke much about the misery of these choices.

As stated in Psalm 14 and in Romans 3:10, there is proof that humans are sinful by nature, and it is everywhere. Due to sin, we have been affected by ruin, misery, desolation, and destruction. Our sinfulness has led humanity to sadness and pain along every path we follow.

No one wants to feel the pain a dishonest and uncommitted spouse placed upon them inadvertently and unexpectedly. Unfortunately, there is little we can do to change the minds of our spouses when it comes to their version of values and moral decisions leading to the road of divorce. If someone is contemplating divorce, they have most likely discussed it with others and have begun to make a plan of action. If you are on the defense side of divorce, you cannot force the hand of the team against you. You are now the hunted and often the powerless party, especially when it is unexpected. You currently have become the underdog and often are exhausted from the hunt.

It's becoming more ambiguous that people can listen to lies and believe them instead of digging deep and searching wide for the truth. I'm wondering why that is today in our world. I also see such a callus society, mainly in our rising youth. It always amazes me through many stories that I am privileged to hear older teens in high school or college-age students explain their relationships to me. Not much different from the husband and wife facing divorce. How does a man or woman divorcing their spouse have little remorse, regret, and feelings of accountability? The amount of lying and hidden secrets is uncanny. The spouse wanting the divorce can feel instantly justified through friends, family, and even church members who agree with their decision. The best analogy to explain this is that it is like your in-laws taking your car for an alignment. They align the car only to go right when, all along, you only needed a balance. The next thing you know, the vehicle (your marriage) has gone sideways with poor direction. Although I was disappointed with my in-laws at this time, I still would have welcomed their help, but they were biased. It was like a sports competition, and they were the referees. They had taken their son's side no matter the facts, and that is a memorable heartbreak and disappointment that are not easily forgotten. Here is when I felt like I was falling into a well, and there was no way to stop the perpetual fall. Shockingly, some Christians seeking divorce do not have the knowledge and support they need to get through this time. It can be challenging to focus and concentrate alone when your world is upside down, and many do not have the finances to have good counsel or therapy to make it through.

Some of us have a distorted view of God's Word on marriage and live in fear of shame after a divorce. On the other hand, their opposers have decided to find any literary teaching that allows them to bend the truth or use selective Bible passages to affirm their position in getting a divorce. I counsel many individuals who see the light and have redemptive feelings toward life after the divorce. For example, it says in the Bible, "It was also said, 'Whoever divorces his wife, except on the grounds of pronoia (sexual immorality), makes her an adulteress; and whoever marries a divorced woman commits adultery'" (Matthew 5:31-32). Some spouses will read this and think they can get a divorce but soon see that anything outside of adultery (and abuse) is not grounds for a divorce.

As a Christian, I believe suffering is just part of life, and living in a fallen world would be expected; this news is better accepted than fought. Suffering is a necessary evil and can increase a person's ability to survive and make better choices as they move forward. Often, the desperate places in our lives become the most rewarding in life lessons. It does not take much attention to recognize that we are in an era of distressing problems facing our country. Our society has a massive issue with contested censorship, poor censorship for our youth, and what appears to be increasing authoritarianism. None of these things mimic good leadership or role models for individuals, marriages, or our children.

We may think we know ourselves and our identities, like in chapter one, but we do not always know our spouses as well as we believe. After all, the one thing we all possess is our minds; no one can ever see inside our minds because it is a private place where we can hide our inner thoughts. However, if we see a slow and constant change in our husbands' behavior, we must take notice. Some of us do, while others ignore the signs. The slow changes can be a form of manipulation in the relationship, changes directed toward altering our minds. This subtle change in our spouses can lead to us losing ourselves, such as blowing things out of proportion, living two different lives, and making us jealous. I call this the merry-go-round effect. It is easy to jump on and spin but challenging to jump off and remain stable in your surroundings.

When the feelings of losing yourself begin, we are at risk for confusion, second-guessing, dismay, and havoc. Everything changed when I was served with divorce papers in my driveway after being followed home one afternoon. From beginning to end, my husband met me with insensitivity, strong-will, and authoritativeness from all involved during my divorce. I wonder if some men and women need these traits to justify their behavior toward continuing in divorce. Maybe, in some way, this way of consciousness assists in ignoring the pain they are afflicting on the other party.

Sometimes, society gives support in odd ways, such as unsolicited opinions and support to continue moving through life as if nothing happened. Misery loves company. Often, these people lead their prey into divorce by not giving the complete picture of what will be revealed later after signing the papers. Attorneys try their best to make things fair, and we all have different perspectives on divorce. My divorce could have been less acceptable or equaled, and while I am humbled and grateful for what I received after more than two decades of marriage, it was only due to having enough self-respect to walk away. I knew that I did not have to lower my standards to see it as a competitive fight to the dire end. I accepted that I could never win with the amount of money, secretive game-playing, and power before me. I just wanted the battle to end and peace to begin in my life and for my son.

The Bible warns about the changes in people, especially in the last days of this world. There are so many books written as commentary on this topic as well. Men will change, and evil will be upon them. Their eyes will have scales and they will not see the truth. I believe many things prophesied are already in motion. Second Timothy 3:2 says, "People will be lovers of themselves, lovers of money, boastful, proud, abusive, disobedient to their parents, ungrateful, and unholy."

Understand also that money is another game-changer in divorce. In society, some people flaunt their money and want everyone to know who they are because culture encourages this mindset. They believe they are entitled to the best of everything, including attorneys and marital riches, when going through a divorce. I experienced firsthand the power of money in the latter part of our marriage. I witnessed the love of "self–career advancement and rising popularity" becoming the idol in our home with my former husband. Some of society endorses our hardwiring to believe that money is "king." When you know there is an undercurrent of adverse change in your home; it is imperative to have someone of greater spirituality to balance the unhealthy environment. 2 Timothy is pretty clear about money, spelling out so many things you need to be looking and striving for in your marriage, and acquiring more money is not one of them.

A part of the darkness that entered my home was when I saw my husband's handwritten notes in his briefcase one night, showing an account of many months strategizing how to leave the marriage. I gasped first, then tried to regain composure as the darkness filtered through the room like a dark cloud. I was most shocked at how long this affair was at work. The chosen opposing attorneys had prepared well to crush all my hope in the restitution of our marriage. Their mission was to drown out all areas of mercy for the financially imbalanced situation I was wandering through. After all, their job is to find holes and weaknesses for their client to win. In my case, it was to win big and leave morality and godly ethics out of the fighting ring. However, there can be a glimmer of light even in this dishonoring mess.

At the end of the proceedings, the opposing counsel walked away smiling and feeling justified in the divorce outcome. I felt stripped of all my clothing and shamed for not making the money to compete with a man worth a million. This outcome is an illustration of legalistic accounts and why the wealthiest opponent generally favors divorce. After the shame and loss set in, the defendant crawls deeper into a cocoon, seeking peace in the chaos. It becomes the perfect environment for some attorneys to spin weaknesses in court to further their agendas, helping them gain power, get further recognition in the community, and strike havoc while the opponent appears weak. Yes, it is like a chess game, only for the fittest!

My Youth

Growing up, I feared making mistakes and doing things considered wrong. This healthy fear was because of my faith and upbringing to fear God's opinion of me. I tried to avoid going to confession at church because I felt humiliated and so shameful, having to verbalize all the sinful things I had done. I wondered what this man, the priest, must feel at the end of the day, listening to so many broken-hearted people confess their sinfulness. Here is another prime example of knowing oneself and staying true to character, even in a mid-life crisis.

You cannot redo the pain you cause another person, ending your marriage. Self-control is a virtue but also something that binds a marriage forever. Each person in a marriage has the power to eliminate shame placed on the hurting partner of divorce. It is simple: keep your marriage vows and be under self-control even in a divorce.

As a child, I mentioned that I was raised Catholic, and my extended family supported this faith. I often felt I had no one who could understand my anxiety growing just thinking about confession and attending youth group. My self-esteem was slowly withering away because I was coerced to reveal parts of myself that I did not want to share with a stranger. I could not understand why God and I could not converse about sin and forgiveness in my room instead of with a priest. Other people of my faith may have experienced a different feeling toward confession. I am so happy that now, as an adult, I am no longer bound to being forced into confession in that manner, and I understand I can directly pray to God without any middle person having to hear my dirty laundry. I feel renewed and at peace talking with God daily.

On another note, I am Italian, so growing up our family loved to eat and have a good time filled with hospitality for their guests. My favorite dish was spaghetti and meatballs; these are my happiest memories. My aunts and grandmothers were very close to me. It was hard for me when my grandmother passed away because I was only thirteen years old. I had not experienced loss until that moment in time. As my life unfolded as a teenager, there were also more great losses. I have tried to turn their examples into positive experiences and know they have helped form my character by being my role models. For this reason and a sample from my family, I will give you my position on divorce: I believe it is necessary in extreme situations. I do not think that someone who has fallen out of love, is in love with another person, or is incapable of getting along in life are reasons for divorce.

I recently listened to a podcast from Victory Church in Atlanta. The pastor had a sermon on the topic of marriage and family. It was so powerful it brought tears to my eyes. As a nation and society, we have thrust ourselves into hearing and seeing things God did not intend. We often cannot protect ourselves quickly enough from eminent danger as the evil one swoops in so fast. We have the free will to be courageous, take a stand, be a coward, and hide under our skin. We have become desensitized and are too blind to see the goodness God hoped for us—the privilege of being married and becoming parents. We are role models that little ones see, but how do we stand tall in such a fallen world?

Not long ago, I listened to another podcast that spoke the truth regarding the journey of a man in today's world. Men may not always get the training from their fathers on how to treat a woman, the needed tenderness, and the respect that is honored. Many fathers are not present in households today, but strong leadership is necessary in a home. How can our youth be expected to grow up with integrity if it is not modeled correctly at home?

This gap is a real problem for young men today to know the truth that will directly impact the future strength of marriages.

I am not sure who here on earth has all these answers about healing from divorce, but we can unite and begin to uncover them together. Divorce was never even an option for me. I believe it is a sacred union that no man should try to separate. After all, I made that commitment before God. Maybe we as a nation do not have great integrity behind our word. As a nation, many have strayed from God, and the sense of right and wrong no longer has the same value as it once did. Getting a divorce seems so horrific to me, while others move through it as another phase of life that comes and goes. This idea is baffling as my heart and soul were invested in the marriage, and still are. Restoration can save many marriages if we can take the blinders off our eyes and have truly humble hearts.

After my grandmothers both died, I remember my parents gradually beginning to argue more. It was awful to hear two people who love each other become insensitive. I often wonder today if the liability of accountability in marriage lessens when parents pass away, and accountability is not there with parents gone. It almost seems possible that some people wait for their parents to be gone before they begin the divorce proceedings. That level of accountability has weakened. Maybe people feel freer to make decisions that once would have hurt the family if the divorce had occurred. I hoped on many occasions and cried many nights, thinking my parents would separate from one another, partially because of my grandmother's passing. I remember the incredible sadness and lack of positive energy in our home. The constant uncomfortableness, knowing all the values and ethics I had learned till now, made life confusing and compromised. I firmly believe this is where fathers need to step in and help their adult sons make faithful and lasting commitments, while mothers do this for their daughters.

My Parental Family Unit

Things became increasingly awkward between my parents in my first year of college. I traveled down that lonely road for about two years in my head, alone. I never knew when I would come home to my family house and see a sign "for sale" propped in the yard, ending all my happy childhood memories. Thinking deeper, I realized that my mom and dad's sense of joy and hope as a family unit would be gone. It still brings devastation and deep sadness to my heart to think about this even now.

It wasn't long before my father left our family home while I was in college. He lived with a single man from work, and it was hard for me to understand how the loss of my dad's presence for my mother could also bring my father to begin a new life. Things were more complicated than just that. Later, my father came back home, and everything seemed back to normal for years until the cycle began again. Years later, the process repeated itself, and my mother moved out. I think this reveals that being separated puts into motion other consequences that later are revealed. My parents are in their late seventies and are still together after working through their issues. I am incredibly grateful for my parents' tolerance, forgiveness, and strength. However, they are from another time of resilience that we rarely see in uprising generations today because they choose to fight through their pains and differences to stay together with the understanding that faith is obedience.

I know our family dynamics affect not just ourselves or our mates but our children. I will always feel sad in my heart going through those years of my youth, which creates anxiety for many others. I think there is a correlation between increased divorces and increased mental health issues. I see many patients who are divorced and have significant anxiety and depression. I see the similarities between children and adolescents of divorced parents. I worked in mental hospitals for years, where the same issues would present themselves. Broken families often can equal broken people. So many individuals I have encountered have little or no faith in themselves, and divorce adds to this.

The Journey

The journey through a divorce is arduous; I will not lie. If you have children, it's even more complex. I remember experiencing PTSD when the phone texts came in with my former husband's name after our divorce. I allowed others to treat me poorly after my experience during marriage because I thought I deserved it. After the divorce, I had such a challenge finding my place in the world and had so much trouble finding a sense of belonging in my space. I felt stripped of my personality. In therapy, I could barely understand who I was anymore.

Prepare yourself for a tidal wave of emotions but know you will make it out alive. I remember living in my former husband's family's time and agenda, often feeling like my husband made a few sacrifices for our marriage while seeking success in his career. Although I always tried to be available for him, it seemed he had lost interest in me. Now, his life included fancy wines and expensive dinners. Eating together was no longer fun; it was almost like an academic event to get a meal or drink. I had so much regret, anger, and sadness from staying up so many nights crying alone. There was only a sense of obligation where my husband was concerned. These things never needed to happen, which made me feel less than. I still remember when we went out as a family before divorcing. I rarely drink alcohol, and that fact would make the dinner intolerable. I never ordered the right drink with the proper meal, and sometimes, when I did not drink at all, a fight began in front of my son.

I want to reclaim this life with my true self through unconditional love. This love instills reality but also hopes for me. There is no shortcut or "pass" ticket to buy forgiveness. Your authentic struggles will make it all worth it in the end. I think my marriage was a front due to all the blame placed upon me by others. I never felt like this before, so I came to acknowledge this life as usual. I did not see how my husband's bullying affected my soul until later. He would often stand in a doorway with his arms spread from side to side, so I could not pass by him until I listened to what he wanted to say. It was so forceful, and I always felt uncomfortable. I felt singled out for so long, being treated poorly by this masked man who seemed good in front of others yet behaved differently with me. Until recently, I did not know that others also saw what I experienced in my marriage. Finally, some rectified emotions while others consoled me with a common truth.

The Pain

I know the pain when your child has been pulled away from you and left with the other parent. At the same time, you sit helplessly as their mother/father, not understanding how this unnatural separation affects you during custody battles. It can be a grotesque act to allow a 13-year-old to decide on having one parent over the other as their caretaker. This atrocity happens every day in the United States. Family courts seem exhausted, leading down a road of insusceptibility to parents losing custody of their children from a divorce.

This concept reminds me of two women in the Bible who were fighting over a child. It is a story in the Old Testament about a wise ruler named King Solomon, known for his intelligence and ability to increase Israel's wealth. In this story, two women are arguing over which one is the mother of a baby. It's a sad and long story, but the gist of it comes from King Solomon's statement:

> This one says, "My son is alive, and your son is dead," while that one says, "No! Your son is dead, and mine is alive." Then the king said, "Bring me a sword." So, they brought a sword for the king. He then ordered: "Cut the living child in two and give half to one and half to the other." The woman whose son was alive was deeply moved out of love for her son and said to the king, "Please, my lord, give her the living baby! Don't kill him!" But the other said, "Neither I nor you shall have him. Cut him in two!" Then the king ruled: "Give the living baby to the first woman. Do not kill him; she is his mother." When all of Israel heard the king's verdict, they held the king in awe because they saw that he had wisdom from God to administer justice. (1 Kings 3:23–28)

Although the moral of the story is that the true mother would not want any harm to her biological child, this story reminds me of how ruthless some people are in divorcing their children watching every poor dysfunctional move. All children need to be nurtured to grow and have respectable character-building traits. You can't just split a child in two, as 50/50 is not always the wisest choice for them. I remember waking up on many Thanksgivings and Christmas's without my son. I could never compete with the travel of flying him to Vail to ski or taking him to literally as many roller coaster parks in a week throughout the United States. I could not buy BMWs, virtual reality headsets, or $1200 iPhones. I think that when I realized the playing field was not fair, my PTSD heightened. It seemed surreal that someone I had exchanged wedding vows with could ever manipulate the situation and tell my son this was a usual way of life. It is not normal, and God hates divorce.

Get your band-aids out and bandage up. We all need one sometimes to help stop the slow bleeding of the destruction caused by divorce. We must focus on what makes us calm in difficult times instead of what makes us sad and has a slow leak towards depression. Many things may be out of our control regarding our children during and after divorce. They may spend more time with the other spouse or friends they can identify with while you cannot. There can be control issues that arise in your behavior or theirs.

So much is lost during divorce. It seems better to try to hold on and control the last things you can. You may be a victim of alienation, constant emotional abuse, and financial manipulation. It is not okay, and God sees all of this. It is not your time to be judgmental or vindictive. I recommend believing that God has you in the palm of His hand. After all, he knows our hearts at all times.

I know firsthand about panic attacks caused by these issues, so I try to teach mindful techniques to most of my clients, using their free five senses with great focus to ease their pain. Touch is the first one. If you have an old silk scarf, packing bubbles, a rabbit's foot, a smooth rock, or a tangle, set it aside for our project.

Next is the wonders of our sight. What are pleasing reminders of happiness for you? I use the memory or image of a charming vacation, silly photos, or a favorite memory to help change the tone of the mood. Then there is our detail to listening. The sound is so bright; there is nothing quite like a beautiful voice singing or a musical instrument in harmony. Then, the smelling and tasting are easy. Think about your favorite candle burning or the scent of chocolate chips baking in the oven.

All of these coping skills need to be in your coping toolbox. To stay sane and have serenity, use what God has given you. Inside, many good items are stored for you to use during despair to soothe your inner self through the five senses.

Toolbox 6:

- Beware of in-the-moment desires; they can change your life's path and break your family.
- Allow God, not society, to push you through to a new level of challenges and success.
- Know that "nothing stays the same." Change is inherent and can also be good.
- Today, the Family Courts seem exhausted or immune to mothers losing custody of their children in a divorce.
- Unnatural acts of separation affect you during custody battles and can weaken you.
- Self-control is vital and helps the pain that can linger.
- Use your five senses to heal. They are your friends and have excellent coping skills.
- You cannot redo the journey of pain that another person has caused you, but you can pray for them to heal along with you.

Chapter Seven

The Many Broken Pieces of Our Children

The ripples of a messy divorce can distort reality and rapidly deconstruct children's minds. I was blessed with one child, and keeping him safe from the undulations of divorce was a job for a village. My child always knew that I loved him to the moon and back until one day, everything changed. It was the beginning of the rough journey that I had prayed that I would never have to walk.

My child was the first to tell me that his father sat him down and discussed divorce before I knew it had begun. That day, my former husband had shown him on the computer that he could legally leave his mother or father in Georgia. Then, he further explained that at age fourteen, my son could choose to live primarily with his father. His decision exemplifies cunning exposure and pre-planned schemes our former mates can put in our children's heads. This manipulation often alienates one parent: I'm a prime example here. I felt like hundreds of sharp-edged knives were inserted into my back, and the air was removed from my entire body as if I was dying. I think a big piece of me did die that day.

I was speechless when I answered the phone while walking in the grocery store that same day, and my son told me to please hurry home. I wish I had recorded the fear in his voice. He was just a kid and should have never had all this adult information dumped on him without my presence. I felt like I would not live through my painful heart racing like a ticking time bomb. My heart rate increased, my hands shook, sweat began to run down my face, and my tears had no stopping point as I felt the confusion sing in my mind. I wondered what person would be so thoughtless to put these harmful and hateful ideas in a kid's mind. My son still remembers the day that his Daddy told him he was leaving! What an awful image for a 12-year-old to bear.

As I entered our once beautiful and safe home that my minister and many other elders had formerly prayed over, I felt the thickness of Satan and pure evil lurking at the side entrance. Within minutes of hearing the news from my son, the home seemed like an empty shell, with each sweet memory being sucked out. It was now a resemblance of another broken family home, with a relator sign beginning to pound into the ground the next day. I understood that someone new would soon live in our home due to our wrecked marriage. He would sell the house, and everything we once shared would be divided or trashed to keep the memories from causing more internal damage to our family. As I sat down to catch my breath, my world shook and was vivid upside down. It seemed the sun would never shine again. My husband refused even to look or speak to me as he begged our son from across the room to come with him and get into the car.

The most honorable thing I will never forget is my son's words, "I want to stay with my mommy," (and he did while his father drove off for the weekend). This outcry made me remember how he often left my son and me every year to hang out at his old college with friends for homecoming games, never asking my son or me to join in the festivities. Even when we were newly married, I remember standing at the door crying as he drove away without a care. For all my married life, he did what he wanted and asked for forgiveness later. There never was empathy.

After the sound of his engine was long gone and the hours passed, I felt like I needed my son to understand that divorce did not need to be wrong. What a lie! I was begging God for me not to drown in sorrow and loneliness. It appeared that my only hope of restoration as a married Christian wife had evaporated. Watching my child trying to make sense out of many messy nights filled with loneliness and uncertainty about our future with his dad gone all the time was too much pain. The fear was almost too much to bear, knowing I would soon be a single mother and no longer a wife.

I cried many nights, holding my son in the guest bedroom and confirming everything would work out. I went to work with swollen, red eyes on many days. My job at the time was serving our local community in churches, hospitals, and private practice for 3,000 hours to gain my clinical mental health counselor license. Ironic, right? I still will never fully understand the strength of God getting me out of bed, dressed and ready for work, dropping my son off at school, and able to put on a facade smiley face that everything would be okay, even when it was a daily war with my former husband spinning everything he possibly could. I would think about my son throughout the day and wonder what I could do better to protect him from what was ahead. My biggest hope is for him to go unscathed through the upcoming divorce. However, I hated that he would now have his own sad and disoriented viewpoint of Christian relationships, marriages, love, and lack of genuine, faithful commitment.

After my former husband served me with the divorce papers, the predators began to come out of the woodwork, spinning my life like a toy top on a hardwood floor. First, my former husband was privileged to stay in the marital home until the final divorce proceedings. Ladies, please do not ever allow this; I was not savvy enough about the damages that would be unleashed during this process to stop this. I often felt like I was living the life of a pitbull forced into a cage where my death was imminent. It was unbelievable that this action was even legal, him staying in the home. I prayed for a quick change. Nothing changed, but the entire process will remain in my son's mind, and my mind, forever. The stick broke the camel's back and unleashed pure tragedy.

Most of the trauma remembrance came from my son and I trying to live in the same house as my former husband. The air was so thick and filled with negativity. This feeling went on for months as I begged the attorney to have him removed. I took my son out on weekends as much as possible, so we did not stay in the depressing house. I dropped my son off at my wonderful Christian friend's place in the neighborhood many Sundays to attend church, as I had to work to have any extra cash flow. Here is where the discord and shame began entering the picture for me. I felt no longer interested, excited, and a pretty wife. Eating most dinners alone was brutal, leaving constant messages that went unanswered and never knowing who or what held my husband's attention. I still remember being in Arizona for a week of business training. It was so hard to get a signal on my phone. I sat crying and unable to talk with my son for a week. The distancing was more than depressing, and the anxiety was unrelenting.

Know that we are generally tied to our past in one way or another. When I would pull up in the driveway and see my former husband open the door of his Land Rover and take my son for the day or weekend, I instantly felt so sick, enduring dry heaves and constant migraines. Seeing this made me physically ill and added salt to past wounds as a triggering incident. Removing a parent from the nuclear home adds chaos and creates a sad and confused child. God did not intend for our families to be this way.

Once upon a time, there were appropriate boundaries supported by two parents. Now, the support and union are lost forever. Our different values led to varying boundaries in the two households. There is no continuity. My son's life journey would never be the same again with rich faith and ideals that would follow the family tradition. Although I know other children experience worse situations from divorce, watching my only son go through this is still challenging. Seeing the damage this caused was especially difficult because that same child is whom I didn't get to hold for months after giving birth to him. Whose hand I had held while he was on life support the night the doctors disconnected his ECMO machine. The same child that I pondered on for many hours, wondering if God would spare his life. With that in mind, nobody's child deserves the detrimental effects of divorce.

Ladies, buckle up. We have no idea how a child will process divorce; each experience is unique. Statistics show the lasting effects of divorce, with higher levels of shame, depression, and anxiety for children. Author Wayne Parker's recent 2022 article, *Key Statistics About Children from Divorced Families, What Research Tells Us About the Effect of Divorce on Children*[iv], states that "There is a 16% increase in the risk of behavior problems if the child is between 7 and 14 years old when their parents' divorce." Additionally, a 2017 study found that children living in intact, nuclear families are about half as likely as children in step, blended, or one-parent families to have a mental disorder or need psychological help. These are astounding statistics that nearly half of us are predisposed to, requiring additional emotional and psychological support due to divorce. I believe that divorce changes the trajectory of our children's lives as well. As children of God and as mothers, we are responsible for better understanding how divorce changes our children and what we can do to alleviate the damage in the process!

Shame, as mentioned in chapter five, generally begins in our youth. It can live with us forever or be let go if we can focus on healing from it. Below is a list of items shame can stem from. This list is essential to know because, pre-divorce, many of these shaming activities are modeled by parents, hence changing our children's way of handling shame.

Here is my idea for a recipe of shame:

1. Yelling and screaming
2. Contradicting one another
3. Stonewalling each other
4. Trying to split the child in half
5. Trying to make the child your friend
6. Trying to make the child choose a side
7. Witnessing parental abuse
8. Feeling emotional sadness and despair in the home
9. Keeping the child in the home with both parents fighting pre-divorce

Below are various dysfunctional outcomes for living in a home with a man who hates the mother of his child:

1. Abandonment issues
2. Over-compensating personality
3. Constant fear and anxiety
4. Exceeding depression
5. OCD behaviors

6. Lack of trust and authenticity
7. Loyalty issues
8. Alienation and being made to hate one parent
9. Risky Behaviors[vvi]

All these minimizing and covert behaviors mentioned above can form and shape our children's outlook on marriage. For some, divorce pain is impossible, and we forget that little eyes are watching and learning from us. I am certainly guilty of this, hence the shame and guilt surrounding me for years after the divorce. It took many therapy sessions to finally understand that I needed God to step in for emergency overload correction from all the shaming in our dysfunctional home before, during, and after the divorce.

Journey in Therapy

My journey began as I rubbed my hands on the soft chenille throws on my counselor's sofa. As I wrapped them around me tightly for a sense of security, the warm tears collected a puddle on the carpet, and it seemed as if they would never stop rolling down my face. It almost seemed that I had been preparing or rehearsing for a character in a nightmare movie. I would get lost in my thoughts, trying to discern the reality of my present moment from all the spinning of truth in each session. I could not see a way out without feeling guilty and shaming myself for having my child in the middle of such a mess. I wanted to have a stronger voice.

I mutedly heard what the counselor was saying as I looked over at my husband, who was relaxing next to me as if he had the best day possible, knowing things were ending. I knew she understood my pain, as she had endured a messy divorce after years of struggle. I daydreamed sometimes with her about what things could have been if we both had left sooner. Those thoughts gave me deep peace about how my son, and I could have lived extraordinary lives together.

After several weeks of therapy, I pulled up the blanket that consumed my tears and cleared my throat, to say the most profound thing ever. When my husband did another no-show, I knew he had planned this for quite some time. Coming to therapy was just a show for him, somehow placing focus on him acting like a Christian by trying one last time to help his wife, the victim. He never intended to bring restoration into the marriage. Every receipt I showed during sessions of the hideous amount of money spent and late nights that he lied about now could continue, and he still looked like a hero to outsiders.

I knew that even though I advocated for peace, my former husband would force me to stand alone on this battlefield and fight the many enemies he brought forth. How many times would I have to wave the white flag and sign confidentiality documents before there was nothing left for me? There are few words for this; I worked so hard helping my husband set up his business initially, but that didn't mean anything now. I did not win too many legal battles; I was portrayed as the villain as I tried to instill good values and morals in my home.

There were many times after the divorce I felt lost. I pictured being in the woods at night, where I could only hear and see my breath. The aloneness and coldness of the white smoke, which turned black as night, from my mouth would remind me of the marital war that seemed never to end. I would reminisce about one of my favorite authors, Robert Frost, who wrote one of the most misunderstood poems, *The Road Not Taken*. This poem meant so much to me because I felt, as Frost did, regarding a lack of individualism in my marriage. I wanted it to be a sanctuary for my child and myself in all my moments. When Frost reached the fork in the road, he discovered he must choose. And he did, while also professing that one day he would return and take the other route. I know only in heaven will I see where the other road in life would have taken me. It is bittersweet, knowing we chose one way with great courage, and somehow, it took me down a road of grief concerning my child but triumph in ending an unloving marriage.

I prayed that my son would have unquenched devotion and the impeccable values to serve Christ. I felt many things in my marriage were challenging the line of excusing good character-building for bad character-building during and after the divorce. First, I do not believe that a parent is to be a best friend to their preteen or teenager. Second, I think that church attendance and Bible groups are necessary actions to stay in good fellowship with others, and third, I think sex and nakedness are nothing positive to expose a teen to while laughing or minimizing the importance of carefully selecting more appropriate things to watch at the movies or on TV.

I began hating to go to work because of the uncontrollable consequences. While I worked in the hospital during late evenings, I would return to see my child up and watching shows like *Naked and Afraid* and *Duck Dynasty*. While I realize that a mother cannot be a helicopter parent, hovering over their child 24/7, it is a good idea that both parents who are divorcing can still be on the same page of appropriate TV shows for their child. Since my husband tried to do everything opposite to my teachings, it caused tremendous conflict and constant stress to our child. At a young age, my son's father raised him to observe acts of worldliness before his age-appropriate comprehension. People with risky behaviors on national TV are not the merit or standard I was looking for him to learn at a young age. Mocking and making fun of me became the source of entertainment on some nights, from my former husband to our son.

I witnessed the confusion and brokenness in my child, piece by piece. These effects were undeniable, and his detachment from school and me grew deeper and deeper. The consequence of the divorce led to many visits to his school and conversations with teachers about this issue. Unfortunately, failing and low grades are common for children of divorced and recently divorced parents. My son struggled to pass a few classes during the first several school years during the divorce. My stress would rise when I saw the headmaster calling and emailing me. Fortunately, as a therapist, I could advocate on his behalf, as his mother, and as a licensed professional. I found him a fantastic tutoring center, and he continued his improvement for months. God was watching and assisting me every step of the way. There were days I did not think would end, but God carried me working through three jobs while racing from my work to his school or doctor and tutoring sessions.

Later, the courts decided to mandate my son to have therapy. While this can be a beneficial mandate for families, it did not seem helpful then, and my son hated going. My income was $17.00 an hour at the time, and my former husband refused to use his health insurance for our son's counseling sessions. I paid $150.00 per visit to many therapists for the next several years. Ladies, please remember in your toolbox that money is spent quickly in a divorce. If you are struggling financially, you must be proactive and ask in mediation or court for counseling sessions to be paid through insurance or by your spouse. If your husband has decided to break his vows, then at the minimum, he should provide after-care for you to remain healthy, especially when children are involved. My husband bucked up with any help that I requested to try to have a professional counselor. He did not care about the mother of his child and made it abundantly clear to my attorneys, family, and eleven-year-old child.

If you are without assistance, remember that books are an option. Many excellent books exist for women and children on the effects of high-conflict divorce. Women battling these issues can turn to resources like these, which can help if therapy is unavailable in awful circumstances.

Also, you need to know what reunification counseling means. It is when the courts believe a gap must be filled between the parent, who is the elephant in the room and is ostracized, and the child. It is super costly and can take months before fixing alienation. This process is when the court stops supporting the one parent with the most power, manipulation, and money to keep the child from seeing the other parent—as much as they can control. Reunification counseling understands that a child begins to enjoy the parent who can provide the most material things and gets manipulated into thinking the other parent is poor, struggles, is embarrassing, is stupid, and cannot handle proper care for them. It is a lot like brainwashing, and because of this I did not get to see my child enough.

High conflict divorces generally have two types of parents: one who exhibits personality traits of an underdog and the other suggesting narcissism and can sometimes strike with passive behavior. The parent with the most money, often called a "Disney Daddy," may covertly and slowly alienate your child. (This title is also for mothers, though it does not happen often.) Courts know it is a devastating behavior, but many cannot control it. It is costly and hard to prove, which is how narcissists generally win because they manage to pay more for attorneys and their controlling nature. Unless cameras are in the home, the judges will have difficulty deciding action because narcissists easily hide their behavior.

I was able to hire another attorney who understood this tragedy that was unfolding in our lives. She was able to have the courts agree to the reunification therapy. Unfortunately, my former husband refused to pay for my part. He expected me to incur these high-end expenses of $350.00 an hour for therapists on a limited minimum wage income. Only three therapists who were well-known at the time did this type of counseling, putting the pieces back together for children. I spent hundreds of dollars only to watch my son, unable to talk to the therapist in a timely manner, which was a requirement during this time. Essentially, she ended up retiring before we ever began.

The therapy could have changed everything for my son and me. He would have had another adult perspective on what is true and what is not for the divorce, an element of respect introduced to him, and hopefully more education on why he was there in the first place. He was angry at me for many reasons, which I believed most was in running a different household than his father. There were rules and consequences that a tenth grader thought seemed too strict at times, so it was not long before he went to live with his father. There was never continuity at the two homes, and I was rarely backed up or respected as his mother. I cannot imagine how miserable it must have been for my son to see the constant sadness in the household.

Narcissists can try to appear calm and collective, even as they are scheming the next move. The fact that my son and I could not even have one counseling appointment together because it would just be another financial waste that only seemed deliberate. These subtle moves can be the beginning of alienation, which can eventually separate a mother from her child. Depending on your child's age and level of understanding, this manipulation will determine if your child still visits you and if you can experience the many years of your child growing up.

I was robbed of quality time with my son from ninth to twelfth grade for manipulative situations like this. I often felt the cold emptiness as a mother without the partnership of feeling like I still had a child. It is an odd feeling as a mother to feel motherless at some points in life. I walked past my child's room, knowing he would never sleep there again. Throwing away old clothes that he never came back for. Looking for countless hours of scrapbooking and understanding those emotions and experiences can never be relived. There was never a shortage of tears from the battle of not being able to have a voice without having a divorce attorney involved.

In some cases, be aware, regretfully, that you will never see your children wake up every day, notice small growth spurts and make marks on the wall, or have any other luxuries of spending time with them on every holiday when going through a divorce. The courts mandate strict and rigid calendars that must be followed, or they will hold you in contempt. I risked being in contempt to get my son to a good therapist; he was not open to therapy with his first counselor. After the counselor wrote a letter of mutual dismissal, I visited another therapist less than a mile from the house. He seemed perfect to start again with fresh eyes. However, they brought me into court and found me in contempt due to insufficient evidence of the countless times I had contacted my former husband to help me get a new counselor for my son.

These are tricky times during a divorce; you must look out for yourself. You must assist your attorney by having all your paperwork, receipts, and notes in order. You must often speak in person to your attorney, eye to eye, so that you are fully aware of each step needed to win in family court, as it can be brutal. It also helps to rehearse what is required for you to understand. Lacking this was an oversight on my attorney and me not to enforce—which is why we were caught off guard that day in court, where we lost badly about the counselor's request.

Counseling could have been a great tool, but not when your child is shut down and hears constant negativity about the other parent—this only leads to an unwillingness to connect with their therapist. It becomes a financial drain with little hope on the horizon. I had a client years ago; her father had been out of her life for many years and became a very wealthy man during those years. He decided to fight for his right to see his daughter, which the court approved. She was nine then and did not enjoy staying with her father and his girlfriend. Her therapist understood her fear and sadness, but her parents encouraged her to continue with visitations. Her anxiety and depression increased.

When she turned ten, they told her that if she did not obey the courts and visitation schedule, she would have to go to a particular school for three months to be schooled in proper communication and following directions. Cell phones were prohibited, and calling to speak with her mother was limited. It was similar to boot camp for children who refused one parent's visitation. Shortly after, they booked her stay, but the location was not to be disclosed to either parent. Although these measures seem extreme, the reality is that they happen in some states of America. These harsh measures of reunification are excellent examples of when the court follows through with a stiff and forceful hand.

For my child, he ended up seeing three separate therapists, each with a poor outcome. The therapists' letters and verbal summations were that he did not have the desire or interest at the time to be there. You cannot force therapy on a child or teen; they will have little respect for the processor doing the hard work that therapy demands. I tried to change his therapist for a better fit since the courts had deemed me with the final decision-making abilities. If you are paying a therapist for months for your son's therapy, it would seem that a parent would read the email of the child's discharge. At this point, I gave up trying to fight the battle, realizing as a mother, there was only so much I could do alone and without an unending money roll or a team of attorneys fighting non-stop. I am still in the boxing ring even years after the divorce. His family told my son that he no longer had to come to his mother's home at eighteen while still in high school. I was shocked to hear this from my son. Just imagine what type of human would tell their child such a thing, hence why you must review everything with your attorney and understand the legal system.

Reunification can be an excellent source of support. Richard Warshak, is a highly regarded expert in the field of parent alienation, who discusses this in one of his famous publications. *Ten Parental Alienation Fallacies That Compromise Decisions in Court and in Therapy*[vii], explains the many fallacies which often compromise the therapeutic process. Some of these include that children never unreasonably reject mothers. The truth is that mothers can be easy targets and victims, too. Children never unreasonably reject the parent they live with most of the time. The fallacy is that more time does not equal quality time.

Another proven lie is that each parent contributes equally to the alienation process. Why should equal blame be put on a sole parent who has done nothing wrong in their child's co-parenting and nurturing process? When a child rejects a parent, that does not mean the parent is bad or less than. I had reversed cases where children had wicked mothers, and the dad was the victim. The circumstances are so very different in every case.

The last misconception is that alienation is short-lived and is repeatedly associated with a coping mechanism for children. This assumption is certainly untrue. Through the many years of my counseling, I have seen unfortunate cases of adult children still carrying the burden of hate for one of their parents because the other parent brainwashed them little by little. Some children are led to hate inertly and quietly before the divorce. I believe that not all high-conflict divorces have alienation present, but if I were a betting person, I would imagine 70 percent are experiencing characteristics of alienation.

If you are a parent of this sad injustice, please stay in the game. Re-establishment with a child can happen. There are many happy endings out there. Be steadfast and strong. A solid support group is also helpful in many ways to assist in the journey and learning the best ways to maneuver through these divorce ripples. While you may be unable to control all factors of how your child reacts to a divorce, your tenacity, determination, and solid faith can move mountains.

Toolbox 7:

- Academic damage, such as failing school, lower grades, isolation, and rising anger, is a common characteristic for children of divorce.
- I felt shame and guilt years after the divorce. It took many therapy sessions to finally understand that I was not in control, and God stepped in for emergency overload correction.
- We are generally tied to our pasts in one way or another. Just observe this.
- If you are struggling financially, you must be active and ask in mediation or court for counseling sessions to be paid through insurance or by your spouse.
- Take time and choose wisely your therapist or counselor for your child. Counseling could have been good or excellent, but not when your child is shut down and does not find a connection with their therapist.
- As mothers, we must realize that there is only so much we can do without an unending bankroll and a team of attorneys who understand and have experience with parental alienation.
- There are great support groups on this topic, which is critical to understand unless your children are 18.

Reunification therapy is a costly choice, generally $350.00 an hour. People dealing with divorce and alienation must trust this therapy with all their hearts. Be wise and closely monitor possible manipulation from others, which may influence the therapist without your knowledge. You cannot control all factors, but your tenacity and determination with solid faith can move mountains and re-establish relationships with your children even in adulthood.

Chapter Eight

Why Do Men Stray?

If we knew the answer to this question, we all might still be married. It is the million-dollar question. I have great insight as a therapist and have had to sit with many men over the years on this topic. I have heard more confessions than I would have liked to have heard and wished so many times that I had a magic wand and could make things better for so many hurting marriages.

Here are a few truths about why some men stray; you can also reverse the same reasons that may tempt women. When a man is influenced by a younger version of you and a more appealing lifestyle, it is an enticement that can seem too alluring and impossible to ignore. Ladies, please do not marry a man much younger than yourself. It opens you up to so many vulnerable situations. I understand that there will be exceptions to the rule. Even a practicing Christian spouse may have desires outside of marriage. If a man is going to keep ties with a single or married woman without accountability partners seated beside him, things can go in an unfaithful direction in a short amount of time. If your husband owns a company, he will likely be involved in the daily hiring process if possible. Therefore, make yourself known to the employees. A woman can have an agenda that no one notices of subtle manipulation and takes her husband by surprise. A man of great character and faith will not waiver; others may.

A lack of self-control is not the only issue that can lead a man into darkness. Temptation is never far. It works together with a lack of self-control, and masking sneaky behaviors is easier for some men than others. Note to self: When your husband switches his routines and begins having later evenings outside the house, increasing his travel plans, dressing differently, manscaping, sleeping with his phone by his side, changing passwords, and refusing to share them, something is happening to this person deep within his soul. The marital breakdown begins. The devil knows the world of temptation and deception all too well. Never leave a crack under the door for him to come in for a visit!

Here is the part where I remind you to keep your husband close and God closer. Ask God for a covering of safety in your marriage. Join a Bible study, have brunch with other Christian women with solid marriages, pray together, and become intentional in your desire for a blessed and godly marriage. My home is open once a month for a Bible brunch. It has been a very successful mending of hearts for both women and men. These gatherings have provided a safe place to help one another grow and heal.

Unfortunately, broken marriages are common in the United States. Psychology Today [viii], has a worthy article entitled *Is Infidelity Contagious?* It reports new research has interesting results about some married people who find cheating acceptable. To further the insult of marital vows, as much as 5.7% of people lie about their affairs, resulting in approximately six more daily lies.

Getting the help needed for healing can be a quest and a large undertaking. From the beginning, marriage is a process of testing who and what you are made of. The union takes extraordinary time and courage to remain healthy, like being transparent, confiding in, and trusting your mate. Daily forgiveness and understanding that we all are sinful while building each other up and affirming one another is crucial to a healthy, long-term relationship. If we ignore these things, we understand that we are leaving a gap open for unseen, evil acts to happen in our marriages.

While keeping your marriage pure, your courage may waiver, and your stability can weaken, which is why I hope your faith can sustain you if the devil comes knocking. He can twist and turn things quickly while distorting your marriage upside down. I have seen many believing men suffer from bondage to sinful behaviors. They do not always know how to escape. These men may begin picking fights with their wives to make everything their spouses do seem wrong. This act is one of the most significant telltale signs that your spouse's faithfulness is being challenged.

Sometimes, some spouses lose their perspective of right and wrong and think their partner is the enemy. Their shift in perspective is how guilt can be displaced. In their marriage, they seek a third person, who is usually the adulteress, as a confidant and good listening ear. That said, nothing good happens to a married man, or any man for that matter, who is not home with his wife and children after midnight. Take notice and never lose your gut feeling and godly discernment on this matter. If your gut is telling you something is happening, it probably is. Take appropriate action. Some great ideas include preparing regular date nights, sharing alone time at night without children, work, or interruption, discovering new hobbies that you can do together, and having a constant goal of excellent communication, such as journaling together or couple counseling for monthly or quarterly check-ins.

Toolbox 8:

- Truths of why some men stray include lack of self-control, lack of personal values and morals, lack of good teaching of commitment, lack of mentoring in church, addiction, boredom, thrill of being chased, mid-life crisis, lack of understanding the union and bridging as one.
- Our current societal values are diminishing, and censorship is what we see at an all-time low for Christians.
- Gain support and keep your marriage pure through being mentored by strong, Christian married couples.
- Be careful when long nights at the office, intimate and private lunch and dinner with solo staff members, missing church, and Bible studies occur. Such resources are crucial in your marriage.
- Be aware of who works in the office or, if your husband owns a company, who he is hiring to assist him in daily work strategies. These relationships can grow closer and stronger right under your nose.
- Refer your employees and staff to their insurance phone number for counseling. If it seems to be an emergency have someone designated (not your husband) to assist in contacting special mental illness counseling urgency's. Have a dress code for

your husband/owner to enforce at work, (sending home women without bras and proper under garments). This should go without saying. When you are not staying on top of things of this nature, things can grow and fester quickly.

Chapter Nine

When to Let Go Before You Are Lost

Letting go of something or someone you love is awkward and painful, while staying focused on what is happening here and now is more important. Some drown in pain and guilt from excessive work, lack of empathy, reckless sex, gambling, and drugs and alcohol. Compulsions often arise when letting go of someone or something, as it is one way for the mind to soothe the loss. Addictions such as co-dependency can be a challenging trait to quit. Domestication, control, manipulation, and false beliefs can keep you spinning forever. Instead, redirect actions from people who are not suitable for you. Consider the below:

Addictions are easier to give into when you have experienced significant loss, so praying for God to guard your heart and mind during these times is critical. There are times that I have felt like a ghost just going through my daily routine, almost like being in a silent movie and being able to see your surroundings, but there is no good way to communicate. God can protect you against losing yourself, as it will be harder to focus on remembering yourself toward the end, and distractions become very inviting when going through a divorce. Did you know that in just one day on your phone, there are approximately 6,000 to 10,000 messages daily? This proves the world has so many distracting noises that can challenge you to tune into God, or not.

Do we have to let go of our spouses when the sinful nature that began the destruction continues in the relationship? You have the power to discern if you should stay or go. I would pray. Evil desires have great appeal and can often reoccur again and again in a relationship. Does that sound like a healthy choice in life? Have you truly listened to what God has told you to do? I do not have the answer, but I do have some wisdom about being still and listening to what God wants you to do.

Recognizing honorable and godly men is an art. I wish someone, anyone, would have taught me more about how to cultivate and nurture positive and encouraging relationships with men. Maybe, just maybe, I would have let go of my husband when I recognized the emptiness of love in the marriage. It can be a real challenge to our human frailty when godly men do ungodly deeds. Man's sinful nature is perhaps why proper guidance and wisdom before a marriage union is necessary to develop a mental playbook to know when a relationship is good and will withstand typical relationship storms. If you recognize it early enough, such insight could prevent ever deciding to let a husband go. Sometimes, your spouse will force your hand to let go, as mine was. I had prayed so many nights my former husband might lament over such foolish and hateful behavior, but God saw a different path for me.

Hence, identifying unhealthy dating behaviors is vital to your future. By age twenty-nine, I had already experienced many dysfunctional relationships. To avoid this, please do not allow your partner to enable you, no matter who they are; this is not what God designed us for. While many of my mistakes shaped me into who I am today, I recognize that what I had wanted most was to be loved by someone of good character, intent, morals, and values and with a firm Christian faith. As I look back in time, I see the many broken pieces of myself scattered from one flawed relationship to the next.

I have experienced different accounts of finding my true north. When I was in college, my true north was art, which helped me to express those inner feelings that were hard to voice. I loved learning about art, fashion, and all the exciting new trends of the era. Back in my college days, I dated a few men who I believed I was going to marry. A few were from broken homes; by this, I mean divorce was present in the family. Their generational curses were not part of my ideal criteria for a possible spouse that I had longed for. I eventually saw the baggage that some of them were carrying from the stuffed-down hurt divorce had placed on them.

After college graduation, I stayed in Virginia and furthered my career. There was no shortage of men or dating, but finding the right mix of purity, honor, devotion, loyalty, and a man with a Christian heart for God was not easy. I dated exciting and intriguing men for several years. My dreams of marriage never faded. A few years later, I met a man in the military and encountered something very different about him. However, he was not physically there for me and was somewhat emotionally indifferent. We dated a bit until he left on a ship. We wrote back and forth, and it seemed fun for a while, but I missed the presence of a man to hold me, enjoy fun things at the beach, and go to church with me. I prayed things would finally work out for us, but he moved away from the beach to be closer to family.

I found myself doing more soul-searching and defining the desires of my heart. Eventually, the man contacted me from Georgia and wanted to continue dating. I was on cloud nine because he seemed to meet many of the markers I had set for a stable and healthy relationship. I also thought I was more confident in my choice since I was older and wiser, this man eventually became my husband.

Being hasty and impulsive gets a person to a dead end quicker. I do not know where my head was, but I was exhausted from dating and thought he might be the last man I would have a chance of finding happiness at age thirty. I still had second thoughts about this relationship because I was making $90,000 a year and had a great job in sales for a considerable company. I had vowed never to be committed to a position over a person who I was in love with.

Later, I moved to Athens, Georgia, and continued dating him. I was able to transfer with my company, leaving my family and friends behind in Virginia. This physical move improved our relationship, and after several months, we became engaged. Since I had chased him for so many months, this proposal seemed very exciting. I continued working for my company and attended the University of Georgia to finish my master's in criminal justice administration. I obtained good grades and was an honorable student in Virginia. I was able to get special permission to finish up my academics in Georgia. Unfortunately, my fiancé had not secured a job then, so I bought my engagement ring, and we had a small party in an apartment clubhouse to celebrate. It seemed a bit untraditional, but I continued heading forward. Ultimately, I was not hearing my inner voice saying, *this is odd*.

I realized I could not spend as much time with him as I had hoped during the engagement because he lived about an hour away from Athens. I was beaming excitedly, and it was a fun time for me during our fellowship. I thought he was a gift from God that I had prayed for. However, as I reflect upon the relationship, I am reminded that even though I prayed about the marriage, I never once prayed for God's covering on the sacred union. At the time, I did not know what that was and was so excited that I failed at the proper steps to ensure our faithfulness. Ladies, never become so happy or distracted that you forget to pray for God's covering, blessing, and guidance.

Making wedding plans and contacting old friends and family seemed more fun than discerning if he suited me. Sometimes, I felt some level of doubt about the upcoming marriage. There were many struggles with hundreds of decisions related to the wedding. I come from a big family who likes to dance and drink at celebrations; his family does not. I had wanted a band but compromised on a DJ due to family persuasion. Even the champagne toast that is customary in my culture, and many others, caused a level of chaos for his family, leading to stress and tension. Many of my family could not come because I was from Virginia, and much of my extended family lived in New York or New Jersey. The wedding location was in Tennessee, which helped his family, who lived there, and I was trying to make it as convenient for them as possible. I knew compromise would be necessary. I thought having the venue in Tennessee was enough to compromise as most brides use their hometown.

We had a lovely wedding, but the fantasy of love and adventure stopped that night. I remember waking up after the first evening thinking I had made a mistake. He had fallen sound asleep minutes after entering the hotel room that evening. I had imagined a very intimate and exciting night for the both of us, which never happened. We left for Mexico on our honeymoon early the following day, which became a fiasco. We departed Mexico early because my health was so severe that I was hospitalized overnight for kidney issues in Georgia. The idea is that anyone can avoid this. Long story short, he had wanted to rent these tiny, little boats to go out on the ocean. It was January and still cold in Mexico's waters. I needed to go to the restroom after we were on the water for some time, but he refused to bring the little boat back to shore to the bathrooms. Instead, I could not seek assistance in the middle of the ocean, and my kidneys could not take the pressure.

I think I knew after returning from the honeymoon that we were doomed. There were red flags everywhere. I lay in the hospital bed alone, as my former husband was busy calling his parents or doing something else. I thought, what kind of man does not care for his new wife instead and adequately risks a severe health issue? As they do, my nurse even asked me if I felt safe and was being taken care of properly. She sensed something odd about us being newly married and our extreme tension. I could have gotten admitted to the hospital, which probably was the best thing for me, but instead, after two bags of fluids, we left. Maybe if I had stayed and talked to a social worker or the nurse about the incident on our honeymoon, I would have made the detour then. Perhaps I could have seen what an awful start to a Christian marriage this was and would have put better boundaries or supportive people in our path. I knew he was almost five years younger than me, and only later could I see the immaturity and other factors that prevented him from stepping up as my husband, caretaker, and protector.

As our marriage progressed, I noticed he had an unwavering attachment to his family. It seemed the family never entirely accepted that I was from a Catholic background and worried about me being older than him. I felt like I was walking on eggshells many times. It became a nightmare on earth to feel unaccepted by him or his family. I was rarely put first, not even at the beginning of the marriage. Every thought or decision in our relationship had to go through his family. Not once was I made to feel that consulting me helped any validity. My anger started to rise, and I continued living in the dark without an opinion or recognition as a partner or helpmate in decision-making in our marriage. The Bible's message about the covenant between Adam and Eve (Genesis 2:24)—leaving and cleaving to your new spouse—never transpired in our marriage.

After three short years into the marriage, I knew we would never survive a lifetime of marriage like I had hoped for. I wanted to grow old together and have a family. However, I lived with a dumbed-down version of happiness, and honestly, I am still amazed the marriage survived as long as it did. His younger brothers and sisters were all having children, and he was anxious and mad that we had not conceived yet. It was not that I did not want to be pregnant; I had always loved children. We just had such a depraved marriage. Also, I told him of my passion for adoption from the beginning of dating. After a few years of marriage, I brought it up again, but he only had negative thoughts about this idea. He made every negative excuse you could of why people should not adopt. Our relationship was so unsteady that I realized I never wanted a child to suffer in an unloving marriage with little promise. However, he made it clear to my family and me that he would seek an annulment if I were not going to have biological children. We began counseling again at this point in our church, but it became too complicated after several sessions.

Some years later, after all of this mess, I became pregnant. We had one son when I was thirty-nine years old, which was a dangerous time for me to get pregnant due to my age and health. Our relationship was no better, and I felt guilty for bringing a child into a dysfunctional relationship that never seemed to improve. Some days, I felt like I was on a hamster wheel that would never stop spinning.

My child was diagnosed early in utero with the deadly congenital diaphragmatic hernia. I had asked my husband to keep this our secret because I was not ready to reveal the sad news to the rest of our family so close to Christmas, but even that did not last long. We began searching everywhere for hope under the heavens to save our baby. A large hospital near where we lived in Georgia was one of the biggest baby delivery centers for many miles. They were unequipped for the risky surgery for me and our baby then. I still remember the medical staff's exact words, "pregnancy termination," verbalized in a conference room with doctors and geneticists during an informational meeting—I never would have taken this baby's life.

I continued with the pregnancy, and our baby, Romeo, was born in Gainesville, Florida. I gave up many things and moved into a small apartment near the hospital for almost three months while visiting Romeo as he was in the NICU. It was a hard time, never knowing if our baby would survive. I did not feel depressed but was often anxious, wondering what God was planning. My faith grew the strongest ever in that time, though! However, my marriage continued to go south, and we drifted further and further apart emotionally and physically. A part of me thinks the distance was a learning process for what was to come. My strength in God and faith that He knew what was best for me made accepting our divorce's fate easier.

There is a little saying that I like to use: "Disagreement is inevitable in divorce; keeping your dignity is another." Meaning, fighting through a divorce challenges individuals to keep their honor as women of God. There were so many opportunities I could have done something less than dignified to my former husband or the woman who assisted in the betrayal of my family. I thought of writing a letter to the woman's parents since she lived just around the corner from my home. Sometimes, I wanted other family members to know the truth by showing them photographs or sending them letters. I was instantly banned from the entire family after someone mentioned the divorce, and I never heard from his mother, father, sister, brothers, aunts, or uncles again. I did not just lose a husband but an entire family of twenty. This letdown is where I could have turned my back on God, but I decided not to and learned to let it all go. I never could understand how they discarded me so quickly. It hurt, mainly because I love his family and all the children. I liked being an aunt and bought many games, art projects, and presents when we visited them on many holidays and weekends. All of this was gone in an instant. I couldn't be in a state of mind without feeling remorse, but I chose to uphold my honor and character to the highest esteem.

Sometimes, letting go is not your first choice. For me, there was nothing I could do. I had always wanted to let his parents know the absolute truth of the divorce, but most attempts I made before the divorce were rejected. His mother told me that I was living a fairy tale in my mind. My romantic ideal did not include what happened to me; it was anything but. I am still honored and well-thought-of in all my prior relationships. How could this marriage be so different and messy? Whatever my former husband said was the only truth acknowledged. He convinced his family that he did no wrong, which is a memory that may haunt me for the rest of my life.

From a counseling perspective, letting go of someone at the right time is essential. Also, having a good ending to the marriage is crucial; it helps in the healing process and strengthens your sense of identity. It also can assist in better co-parenting styles and other things.

As a Christian, I read the Bible about divorce often and knew I had grounds for leaving the marriage after about six years; however, I still stayed. I would have stayed longer for my son to have a home with both parents. I lived with a blind eye to things for a long time and wished and prayed so many times for God to help our marriage. There was a time when my ex-in-laws wanted us to consult them for help. But when things got terrible, I do not think they truly wanted to hear or believe the situation. I knew they were no longer good referees for our marriage anymore. Ladies, you must understand that not many mothers or fathers will be objective in their child's separation. However, I was proud of my parents during my marriage, as they remained quiet, and to this day, they have never said bad things about my former husband in front of my son. Peace of mind and slowness to anger is God's truth.

When children are involved, you must be smart enough to weigh the pros and cons of divorce, of letting each other go. You need to be on your game and have an intelligent and ethical personal consult with you during the process. If you are being hurt emotionally or physically or are a victim of infidelity, God will guide you with wise counsel on how to proceed. Do not stay in a marriage as long as I did because it only perpetuates the damages to all involved if reconciliation is impossible. And while children can be resilient and come out the other side okay, some ages are worse at recovering than others. Sometimes, it takes years before you begin seeing the damage in your child after a divorce.

Letting go is an actual test of the human spirit. I am in my fifties, and it has taken a third of my lifetime to pick up most of the pieces from the divorce. But I am proud of who God intended me to be and showing me a divine new purpose for my life. I believe that things will work out as they should, according to God. I was very fortunate to have Godly support from various directions, including good mentors and some unexpected faithful people who came into my life at the perfect time.

Toolbox 9:

- Recognizing faithful and honorable men is an art. Try listening to God and the Holy Spirit more often for discernment.
- Healthy communication and a genuine desire for commitment grounded in Christ are essential in marriage.
- Beware of handsome, prideful, exciting, intelligent, and intriguing men. These traits could be your addiction or co-dependency and not true love.
- Sometimes, letting go is not your choice but could be part of an intervention in your marriage. There is hope in your future, no matter the outcome. God already knows your decision and is with you! Slow down and listen. Drown out all the distractions of the world.
- When you are experiencing manipulation in marriage, it may be a sign of control and an authoritarian type in a spouse who never really sees you as their equal half.
- When there are children involved in an unhealthy marriage, you must be smart enough to weigh the pros and cons of getting a divorce.

Chapter Ten

Damage Control and Proactive Behavior

Proper damage control can likely help you during a breakup or a divorce. Here is my knowledge and two cents about the price of loss, which I believe is worthy of hearing. Damage is when something is broken or, worse, purposely destroyed. That was my marriage, so damage control did not stand a chance. However, having the ability to remove yourself from your emotions and knowing that divorce is a sizable money-making business worth millions in the United States alone. When we are on the losing side of divorce, we fight or lie down. I fought with all my soul and heart, even when I did not have the same luxury of parents close in proximity or able to assist me with the endless finances. Money can be the biggest game changer in divorce.

Nevertheless, there are ways for you to control at least parts of the divorce that can be so damaging; and that is by accepting the present moment and what is happening to you. You can gain more control every moment than you may believe by staying calm, collected, and surrounded by wise counsel.

We are not immune from being wounded during life experiences like divorce and realizing that sadness, depression, and anxiety will continue during the problematic battles in divorce. It challenges our beliefs, values, morals, and traditions that we can hold in great esteem. It feels so helpless at times when someone we love tampers with them. My story may sound like a massive, poisonous factory spill to some, and it was (more than I am allowed to write). It lingers in my mind like a bad meal that costs a lot. Custody battles never truly end because of the aftermath—this is another part of a costly custody nightmare. These are things one never expects in a typical divorce setting. Rarely is this the case. Claws come out, and the fight begins. What one parent believes is correct and best for their child is not always what transpires.

Unfortunately, when you deal with men who do not want to embrace their sensitive sides, show remorse and forgiveness, give mercy, or give up control, you will ultimately have a dark or skewed narrative for your late marriage and divorce.

I believe that help from proactive, hardworking attorneys who foresee extreme situations can extinguish them before they implode. My battle cost a pretty penny, including my life savings, due to the complexity and game-playing during my case.

Remember in chapter seven, I forewarned you what happened to my son at age eleven when his father sat him down at the computer and explained every detail about leaving his mother as soon as he was fourteen? I truly felt like Alice in Wonderland. I kept waiting for the reinforcements to break the door and defend the salvageable pieces of this torn-apart family—unfortunately, that didn't happen. So, in shorter terms, damage control is essentially the most critical aspect to have in divorce proceedings to limit excessive pain. You must put yourself first for a time and have an accountability partner to keep you solid and consistent. It takes much vulnerability and forgiveness to keep your motor running smoothly during a divorce. Emotions may be hard to control during divorce, but you must learn to control them to make progress. Think about checking your feelings like checking a coat at a cocktail party. Leave them somewhere safe until you can tend to them.

Damage control includes the devastation to learn that your loved one no longer wants you. It's even worse to discover that your spouse had been planning it for many months. And it's unthinkable if they want to replace you and, with any luck, take your children away. Stopping the pain and suffering from every direction seems impossible during the divorce. It may seem there is leakage in every path of your life that cannot be controlled or contained. You may even feel like you are drowning in an ever-filling pool.

We can feel so devastated when our marriage is in trouble that we do not think clearly. We cannot deny that sadness permeates the neurological pathways in our brains. Our brain is like a machine; we can experience flooding of neurochemicals and hormones dancing in our minds during distressing times. We may feel that any decision is too hard to make or that we live in a constant fog where we cannot focus on what's before us. If we are willing to lean on our trusted friends, faith, and allies to help us, our decisions come with fewer distractions and more intentions. It will never be easy to leave someone with whom you share your most intimate secrets, hopes, and joys. Although not all marriages experience restoration when one party chooses to go, you must be strong and wise to accept that.

We will always have a mental file of the battle wounds from a divorce. Our brain does not just let go of these memories that were assaulting our character. However, damage control can help us reach deep and feel our strength increase to prepare for what is about to begin, changing our narrative to strength and courage. You need to be your best friend during the loss of a relationship.

Take fear by the neck and strangle it! Fear is your enemy, and with it, progress will not happen.

Suppose humans could only be satisfied and grateful for what they have. My parents taught me to respect myself and others. To get married and stay married. Today, things do not seem so straightforward. I wish our society embraced commitments; wow, what a pure and lighted world we might live in with less reason to be guarded and selfish.

These following quotes gave me the courage to take the next step on those frequent days when I thought it might not be possible to move forward:

> "Balance is restored after status quo has been shaken to its core. Just as if a rainbow comes after the storm. Know and be still, there is more of your story to unwind."

> "How very little can be done under the spirit of fear."[ix]

My damage control story began here. I came home one day after working a twelve-hour shift at the hospital. I was still interning in my counseling program when my former husband started the process of leaving our family. I walked into my living room, where his father and college best friend were seated. The odd energy hanging in the air when I walked into the room immediately set me on edge, knowing their conversation was not good, and quickly ceased upon my arrival. No one acknowledged my presence, and instead, they moved the conversation outside to the porch.

My son came running to greet me. We were like two pieces of Velcro, inseparable. I always wondered what he overheard in these secret family meetings. We often just went out to get food to leave the depressing house and its brokenness. The money had stopped coming into the bank account, and I still have no idea where it went. After twenty years of marriage, I had to ask for money each week like a child from my husband. I hated how he had so much control over me regarding money, which was my only survival unless I left the state to stay with my parents. It felt so humiliating to have a need, even just for a meal, going to the doctor' paying my insurance co-pay, taking my son to all his doctor appointments, and paying the deductibles and all the utilities. During the divorce process, but not divorced, my husband often gave my son money for things we both needed but was told it was not me. He would not let him bring leftover meals home. I question how it is good mentoring to exclude your wife, the mother of your child of so many years, and begin teaching a young teen to think that it's okay to grow up thinking that this behavior is acceptable and correct.

Revelation 21:4 says, "And God shall wipe away all tears from their eyes; and there shall be no more death, neither sorrow, nor crying, neither shall there be any more pain: for the former things are passed away."

Damage control comes in many layers. Finances were near the top for what God, and I could accomplish together. I did not see how a woman in her fifties could have an excellent job in today's confusing market and remain financially stable. Moreover, how would my retirement funds be sustained or grow for another fifteen to eighteen years so I could retire? Even though I was working three jobs just over minimum wage, it still was not enough money during the months of divorce for basic expenses. The refrigerator broke and got fixed two months later after all the food was rotten without refrigeration; snakes appeared in our garage and over our entry door and had to be taken away by wildlife; our deck collapsed, putting my son and his friends who visited our home in danger; the house needed many repairs before it could sell, but my husband never assisted in even one house repair: I ended up paying for these services alone. Despite that trial, I can share my truth; God will rescue and restore you. You have nothing to lose at this point. Just have the faith of a tiny mustard seed and watch it grow! I did become more robust out of necessity.

While trying to heal myself, I also received counseling to find the best healing method for my son. He is my only son, my only child, and all I have. I had waited so many years for him to heal and feel secure. God spared him at birth, and he survived the odds with his rare diagnosis. I wondered who I would be without him. The stress seemed constant due to trying to manage my son's health, my physical health, and my mental health. I knew things were changing rapidly and could not continue to ignore the signs. It hit home after unsuccessfully locating my husband before signing papers for one of my child's emergency surgeries. It was frightening and sad on many levels.

On another occasion, I was alone with my aunt when my son was rushed by ambulance from his pediatric office to the hospital while he was turning blue. I remember talking to many of the doctors on his care team about the stress at home and its effects on my child. I felt I had disappointed his primary pediatric doctor because she was always so kind to us, and I was sure she wondered why I stayed in such a toxic environment. She was so upset and angry the day he was rushed to the ER from her office. That morning, my husband did not want to go with us to the doctor. He felt that I was overreacting to my son's condition, then proceeded to put work first, as he had done on many occasions. The damage control seemed impossible for me to accomplish, trying to be a good mother and a working wife while balancing a terrible marriage and a sick child for many years.

I knew that I needed my armor on for the upcoming battle. I remember telling my son not to worry that everything would work out. A mother can never lose her children's trust. They are likely sad and have anxiety-ridden thoughts already. Your job is to calm and soothe your children as this awfulness unfolds.

During divorce proceedings, my former husband and I had two eight-hour mediation days. During mediation, the court granted 50/50 custody, and I had primary parental control of my son for significant decisions. After about a year, my son had difficulty going back and forth to our homes. He was also diagnosed with attention deficit hyperactive disorder (ADHD) and had so much trouble focusing on school and keeping his grades up. His father exercised his decision-making authority by placing my son in extracurricular activities and putting him in the school band, which took time away from his studies and home life. My son was in a private school that was rigorous in academics. When he was with me, he complained about the difficulty of school and finding good friendships. The stress was mounting, and I could see he was internalizing the divorce and not coping well. Seeing the adverse effects of divorce on such a fantastic child made me very sad. A mother can always see the school counselor and try to have any assistance needed for the children. We can also get our children in a Biblical boys or girls church group that reinforces love and connection with peers.

My son did not want to join any church groups during the divorce. His father kept him constantly busy with things that he wanted him to do. He signed him up for something in school that would take over all our spare time to bond. Pick-ups at school became later and later. My son and I began to drift further and further apart. He began to change and disagree on the house rules, became easily angered, and lacked the necessary consistency in rules and boundaries between our two homes. I had zero support from his father, as he refused to ever agree with me when it came to terms of childcare. Every decision I made regarding my son seemed to be wrong and stupid to him. Looking back on it now, my son was emulating his father's behaviors in the home. Beware: There are so many personalities in this world, some of which may never come out until close to the parting of your marriage. If you have married a narcissist, know they love a good game, especially the play of good cop versus bad cop.

Not long after, my son asked the courts to change the custody terms. I never felt so dismissed and dishonored than the day my son signed over my legal parental rights as his primary decision-maker. I could never speak with the judge because the attorneys handled this significant ruling, and Covid had begun slowing things down even further. Imagine your only son, whom you cared for on many levels, would choose to leave you and live permanently with their father. Furthermore, how could a man who did not even know all his child's doctors be allowed the role of the primary caretaker? If you are asking why I didn't fight harder, the sad fact is I never had a chance to compete with my former husband's millions of dollars and expensive lawyers.

That is how generational traumas begin. Undoubtedly, as my son ages into a man, there will be scars of the trauma. I am hopeful he will break generational curses for his children. In the constant tug of war between us, my son never had the authentic opportunity to find his "true north," his path forward. I participated in this; I had hoped he would remember the countless days of fun we spent together pre-divorce. We went to parks, zoos, day trips with friends, train rides, horseback riding, beach trips with my parents, and some of the most memorable experiences of a lifetime. We even traveled to two of the seven wonders of the world. I believed we were so close he would never leave my side. Mothers, hold on to your hats because children may turn on you instantly; after all, their brains do not fully develop until age fourteen, and divorce can sometimes bring bad influences. It can depend on your opponent's strength, cunningness, wealth, and effects on how successful you will be in the divorce.

Everything changed instantaneously with my son's decision. What I had thought I knew about the love between a mother and her son was a lie and is now shattered. My modest living was no match for the extravagance my son experienced when he was with his father. Some sound advice would be not to allow a toxic pre-divorce situation to continue in your home. This toxicity is another example of why we have better damage control regarding divorce and children. Children do not need to see all the messy things that adults do. I am still in shock that my husband at the time was allowed to live in the family home while he had plenty of money to relocate anywhere else. It hurt the Christian character-building I had worked so hard on with our son. I hated that he had to see the dysfunction and poor behaviors of his parents interacting in the same house.

My son had to choose between having holidays with me alone or going with his dad to see his grandparents. My son had no choice but to get in the car on various occasions with his father, leaving me standing in the driveway crying. When they went out to dinner almost every night, he was not even allowed to bring leftovers back for me, even though I worked three jobs and made a minimal income. It became so toxic that my young son began to change from a sweet and humble boy to someone hard for me to accept at times.

I understand as a mother that we all have those teenage years, but there was something far more happening with my son. I explained that chasing after the narrow gate will lead you to a better life with peace, love, joy, and self-control. Doing so can supply true fulfillment and flourishing faith.

For example, my son left my house on the afternoon of his sixteenth birthday. It was my year to have him on his birthday, but instead, he joined his dad with friends to celebrate at one of the most expensive restaurants that most adults cannot afford. Moms do not beat yourself up because someone appears to be robbing your child's affection. Boys may choose a lifestyle that looks better than they can provide as a single mother. Remember that no former husband can steal your title as a mother, even when it does not seem like anybody cares. God gave you this title and gift for a reason.

Regarding damage control pointers for advice during divorce, if you are responsible for paying for therapists, ensure that insurance will pay in your court papers. Counseling is a costly undertaking and can last for years. You should not find yourself in a self-pay situation. I paid for my son's therapy for several years, and not one of the three therapists was in the network, with rates ranging from $150.00 to $175.00 a week. My son had excellent health care insurance from his father but was not allowed to use it for therapy, as my former husband thought it was unnecessary. One more hidden secret: my son hated it, and I never saw behavioral improvement. He was so angry, and I tried to switch him to another therapist, but that only backfired.

My son stood by while his dad took me to court and sued me for discontinuing one of his therapists and finding another therapist closer to our home who specialized in his age. He and his dad won that battle and many more. His dad got control of who my son would see as his therapist. This man would be sharing very intimate conversations about our lives. I was a therapist and knew how imperative it was for them to have a good, authentic working relationship in counseling; however, this never happened. My son would go when his dad felt like enforcing it but ignoring it all the other times. Things were so inconsistent for my son. They both played games, one after the other, in the legal system until I stopped trying. I pulled my heart out, dug a big hole, and put it deep in the ground for safekeeping.

At this point, I could accurately discern this was no longer a family, and I was alone. I had lost everything in this war and never felt safe around them again. I knew what it felt like to lose your innermost dignity. I had to keep my life private and act as if everything was fine so I could still perform in my job. My son would leave the room emotionless whenever I tried to talk to him about what had happened. Anytime I shed tears or wanted to discipline him, he walked away. He reacted no different than how his father had modeled to him throughout the years in our unhealthy and unloving marriage.

When threatening memories come to your mind, you must have strong guardrails to keep yourself on track and focused. Otherwise, you will drive yourself crazy, so I urge you to replace them with something positive (refer to Toolbox). My way of managing this for many years was to replace thoughts of chaos with soothing times of joy. I remember when my child was in the hospital for almost three months—he once had so many tubes winding in and out of his tiny body that I feared holding or touching him. When he got close to coming home, and the lines started to come off, I would put my hand out, and he would squeeze my fingers with a firm grip, like he was saying, "Never leave me." I was there every day at the hospital for him. I would imagine what a wonderful son he would grow up to be. These memories comforted me in trying times.

Another tip for your toolbox on healing through damage control is to compare your pain of the divorce or the aftermath to something else that hurt more, which you made it through (refer to Toolbox). Nothing could replace it when my son's surgeon came into my hospital room near midnight and sat down. As I remember, he asked me if I wanted to sit with my son before they removed the life support to prevent compromised brain function from being on life support too long. Thankfully, it was a true miracle, and my child was able to breathe on his own. No one could speculate how long a day or a lifetime his excellent health may last. Birthdays became meaningful, and daily life with him, waking up to face another day, seemed spectacular. After getting through that, I believed I could withstand more than what the divorce could ever throw at me. Galatians 6:9 states, "Let us not become weary in doing good, for at the proper time we will reap a harvest if we do not give up." Also, in the apostle Paul's teachings in chapter 6 of Galatians, I believe he wanted others to understand the purpose of living in God's sovereign spirit to overcome difficult situations.

Learn to let a toxic marriage go before cancer eats at you. It still makes me cry and sick inside at the thought of how bad those years were. As mothers, we may suffer during and after a divorce with our children's reactions. Just know you are the adult, and they are trying to figure things out. You may not receive an apology for something significant but have grace. Fighting with your child only gets you more legal issues and another lost custody battle. My son would visit one or two days a week, as included in the court arrangement. They gave me hope that some mandatory sessions with a counseling specialist in alienation and family restoration could help us. I remember paying for several sessions at $250.00 each. Then, my former husband took so long to complete his part and did not encourage my son to attend in-person sessions despite the court's mandates. One day, the therapist called to inform me that she had waited long enough for sessions with my son that never occurred. She decided to retire and withdraw the case, but there was no return on the investment. I could not start the process again, and my former husband was not supportive of the arrangement.

This type of failure to complete something important in a child's life is unnecessary. No one has to take this silence, lack of respect, and abuse in or outside a marriage. God will not fault you for leaving this type of marriage and will give you the tools and people to help you heal! Let's face it; you will probably be healing for many years after the divorce. It is a horrific and mind-bending experience for most, especially those with infidelity. That is about the cruelest way to end a marriage, but you can move forward again. I always liked the following quote about signs of gratitude and hope by William E. Gladstone, a British statesman and liberal politician. He served twelve years as the United Kingdom's prime minister in a career lasting over sixty years.

"Be happy with what you have and are; be generous with both, and you will not have to hunt for happiness."[x]

Sometimes, using a notebook to jot down everything in life you can be grateful for, or a glass mason jar filled with good memories you experienced is helpful. Journaling will help in damage control to stay focused and calm. It can help with depression and even anxiety. I have also come up with hundreds of art therapy ideas, which seem to boost the spirit and allow the stronger you to come out and play a bit. One of my favorites is buying Wish Paper online. They are thin sheets of small paper you can write on, listing things you want to manifest. Then, you light the form with a match, and it whistles and whizzes through the air as it quickly burns out. Another fun idea is making a cigar box filled with your favorite coping skill ideas. I add one thing I like to touch (fabrics, scarves, a rabbit foot), several things to smell (samples of perfumes or spices like a vanilla bean), my favorite candy (a few pieces of gum), and pictures of meaningful people or places to look at. These help in getting you focused and calm.

Toolbox 10:

- You will always have a mental file of what happened during your divorce. Do not let it be a dark memory that is easy to recall and brings you to places of despair.
- Damage control is the most critical aspect of getting good healing. You must put yourself first for a time and have an accountability partner to make it through. One of the best things during the divorce is not allowing your almost-ex to live in the same home.
- Change your narrative to strength and positivity instead of doom and gloom. That is for victims, not you!
- Emotions may be hard to control during this divorce process, but you must learn to control them to make progress.
- When your husband switches routines and begins having later evenings, increasing travel plans, dressing differently, manscaping, and sleeping with his phone, something dark is at work inside.
- Join a Bible study, have brunch with Christian women, pray together, and become intentional in your desire to have a blessed and godly marriage if possible. You can also do these things if you are going through or overcoming a divorce.
- Have daily forgiveness and understand we all are sinful. Build each other up and affirm one another.

- Notice and never lose your gut feeling and godly knowledge about your marriage and what a marriage should be.
- Not accepting the truth quickly enough about your current situation with your spouse can leave your marriage too far gone.
- Have a special box that you make with good rescue items inside, like something good to smell, touch, and read, and a few great pictures that might be of a place you intend to go and relax after the divorce is over.

Chapter Eleven

Is Healing Really Possible?

Yes, yes, and yes. It is possible to heal! It is like threading a needle — it may take a few tries, but with the right motivation, it will happen. I am not sure we will ever be able to understand how some people do actions to one another that can diminish our godly society. It seems their purposes are without merit and makes me wonder, as a therapist, what is going on in the minds of these people. After being beaten down, called every disrespectful name, and made to feel useless and unloved, you will return to the restored truth of who you are and how God sees you. Based on observations through my practice, women tend to be the easier targets for divorce after falling in love, getting married, and having children because of being sensitive and emotional. Many of you are familiar with this story.

Resistance to physical and mental harm to another, especially a spouse, is a superpower that some of us are unfamiliar with. Divorce drains us of our natural ability to collect and retain our strength, stealing our joy, distorting our hope, and leaving the brain so exhausted that it cannot think clearly. We often feel exhausted for many hours of our day, which can lead to depression. And along with depression comes its best friend, anxiety. This combination makes a living seem impossible at times. Divorce depletes much of our natural and wholesome energy, so it is imperative to have a good physician, therapist, exercise program, support system, and psychiatrist if needed during a divorce. Faith is the best part of your support system, the ultimate spring of rejuvenating your healing.

Faith in God and each other keeps a balance in marriage, helping partners to respect each other and to build a truthful foundation for a healthy relationship. With steady faith in each other and God, authentic love enters the relationship freely. Your vitality of forgiveness depends on your faithfulness and optimistic perspective of growing strong together. Anyone can start fresh in a marriage if they use the proper components—faith and love. However, reminiscing is not when things are over, and there is no hope of reconciliation. You must choose what thoughts can take space in your mind. They do not pay rent, so eliminate the ones not helpful for healing. A good rule is that if the thought is not godly nor faithfully serving you, then delete it from your memory. These unhelpful thoughts are often called irrational thoughts and can surface after a divorce. Some ladies share with me that they have never needed a psychologist or psychiatrist, yet often feel they can no longer control their emotions after a divorce. This type of reasoning seems to bleed into their employment, friendships, family interactions, and so much more in an unhealthy manner.

During divorces, many spouses inflict manipulation by making the other person feel unhealthy or crazy; this is a lie. For instance, my husband called me many names and even called me crazy. It is so hateful and demeaning of someone who once felt love from their spouse for so many years to say this to their wife and mother of their child. Many clients need an extra healing stabilizer due to their spouses' pain. It can be so intense when they are going through a divorce. Many of my clients report wanting to return to their normal baseline of who they used to be. They have told me they take anti-depressants and anti-anxiety medication to assist them through the egregious war.

I believe that taking psychotropic medicine, even short-term, gives many women a fighting and fair chance of defense during a turbulent divorce. The medication helps when you are overwhelmed to take the edge of anger, agitation, and sadness. Due to high, stressful times, your mind processes slower, and you can become unmotivated and sluggish. However, the medicine can give you some power over your life that you may have temporarily lost. Things will not quite feel as gray with these medicines. I was fortunate that I was able to remain stable during the entire process of my divorce. However, there were days when I thought I might not live to see the next day due to the stress.

A daunting day that remains etched in my memory was when I was with my son, and my attorney called to ask permission for opposing counsel to access all my medical records. They were looking for any narcotics and anti-depressants I used. It was a low blow, trying to uncover any evidence of instability to use against me. I had an ankle replacement, where I could not walk for six months; back surgery to replace L4 and L5, where they removed my bone out of my body and replaced it with metal rods; an emergency C-section for my son with his life-threatening diagnosis; and a tummy tuck after the birth of my son where I have a 22-inch scar from hip to hip. I am unaware of any woman who might undergo these gruesome surgeries without prescriptions. While homeopathic medicine is and was my preference, I am all too aware when people abuse drugs—causing addiction. It breaks my heart that during divorce, a spouse will shame their partner as a drug-seeker when they are correctly using medications.

Since my son was a young boy, he suffered from bad headaches. His babysitters would call me at work and ask me to come home quickly because he was on the floor holding his head and screaming in pain. During the divorce, my son complained of migraines coming back. His father had never met the specialist doctor I had taken our son to often, but the new divorce orders stated that he must know about all doctor appointments. Suddenly, my son's father became available and attentive to the doctor appointments that he had never shown the slightest interest in, and he attended this appointment for my son's migraines. At a meeting for my son, which he had never been to before, my former husband told the neurologist in front of him that I made him feel he had migraines so that I could take his medication myself. This accusation was so far from reality, and I honestly did not understand what hateful thinking could make a person do such an atrocious and deceitful act. I could make my appointments to get help if I needed any medication.

Untrue accusations can become a breeding ground for other painful instances and memories to surface. When I was hospitalized and preparing to give birth to my son, they placed my husband and me in a room with an administrator. It was a safety measure for the hospital; should the delivery go south; they should first try to save my life. He checked the box, said no, and declined.

All of the last-minute stress did not permit me to have an epidural. Instead, the doctors administered medication to paralyze my entire body except for my eyes. I could only blink. My anesthesiologist was by my side and held my hand. He was the only human interaction I had during the birth; as tears ran down my face, he wiped my eyes while my husband stood, checked out, somewhere in the room. What I imagined to be a glorious day for two married people having a baby was anything but. I could not find peace or comfort that day or possibly any day since then.

One can find healing from several different approaches when you're undergoing pain and betrayal. Medication can partially numb you when the pain is intense, as with other ways. I did so much personal grieving alone at my house that it could have floated me away like a ship to any country. I did not have a family to support me physically. During the first year going through my divorce, I saw my parents only once; that made me sadder that they were not there for me. I had a huge house and needed someone who loved me to be there and share their time with me. That would have meant the world. There were times leading up to the various court dates when I needed the presence of my parents or loved family and friends to stand with me.

During my grief, I worked out my eyes and tear ducts and wondered if I might need a new pair of both, but healing from the inside out, especially with tears, is one way of cleansing. There is so much toxicity after a divorce that we must find a way out. Healing can go through many stages of emotions, which can feel like setbacks. Sadness and aloneness are the main ones, but there are also the emotions of anger, jealousy, grief, and rage, to name a few more.

Writing this book was a source of healing. I wanted to help others see that the venom of a snake bite does not kill the strong. You will get back up and enjoy your life, especially when you can reconcile that your marriage was just one chapter of many more to be written. Without all the support I received through this awful loss, from what seemed to be never-ending pain, I would still be trying to figure out how to move forward. A dear friend took me to a twelve-week Divorce Recovery class. Many churches offer a course to help divorced individuals heal with God and breathe again in life. She sat with me many nights, saw many tears, and empathized with my pain. I wanted to pay it forward like she did, so I ended up sitting through the classes with another sweet lady. Right now, if you are in the process of divorcing or are recently divorced, you either need to look for one of these classes or try to help another get through the process. A prayerful community enables you to take the focus off your issues and toward helping someone else.

During the divorce, I was diagnosed with complex post-trauma system disorder (CPTSD). For those who do not know the types of traumas, please let me explain. There is acute trauma that comes in quickly and ends pretty abruptly. Another type of this disorder is chronic mistreatment, where the brain cannot process why this is happening (in my case, from a loved one I had trusted for many years). This diagnosis results from what we have discussed regarding verbal and physical abuse. The pain is prolonged and may seem never to end. Then, there is a complex post-trauma system disorder, which is what I have. The pain kept coming daily. My emotional system was a train wreck and always seemed to be triggered by even looking at my phone and seeing a text from my former husband.

Another characteristic of CPTSD is when you are constantly anxious, wondering when the next bomb will drop, or the next issue will hit. I knew my mind did not work like this, and happiness was my true center of calmness. I was not used to being purposely hurt and accused of truly ungodly things. It made me feel like someone was watching me. For example, one morning, an unfamiliar car sat to the left of my driveway as I left for work. I called my private investigator, and he put a trail on the car. Unfortunately, we never found out who was in the car that morning. All I know is that he looked me right in the eye, and it gave me chills to think about what he may have had in his mind. It seemed as soon as I could come up for air, there was something else to crush me. I feared the most minor things that reminded me of this man. I avoided certain restaurants we used to go to, places we used to shop, parks we used to go to, and so much more. I felt I could never heal or catch a break, as this ordeal frightened me and was difficult to accept. I could not see a calming and restful environment except alone in my house, and I still felt attacked even there.

My experiences are similar to those of other women who battle with PTSD and CPTSD. In that, these specific individuals become "frozen in time", as Courtney Armstrong puts it in her book *Rethinking Trauma Treatment: Attachment, Memory Reconsolidation, and Resilience*[xi]. Consequently, causing them to struggle with moving forward in life, as I experienced. Armstrong also mentions how "PTSD is a disorder of memory integration between three levels of our triune brain," and how the reptilian brain and mammalian brain hijack the cerebral cortex when we are in a highly aroused emotional state. This hijack raises concern because for it to "Mobilize a survival response... All our logic goes out the window." Understanding these facts about PTSD should urge us to combat it as strongly as possible. However, it is unfortunate that many women don't always understand the benefits of therapy and repeatedly talking through their traumas with a professional. If I could tell them one thing it would be: Doing so is particularly important because this practice of memory consolidation makes sense of trauma by "recalling the implicit memory while simultaneously evoking a new experience that changes the meaning of the memory and invalidates negative beliefs attached to the trauma event."

Similarly, I felt frozen in my thoughts many times. For one, I was not the best communicator and secondly, I felt outsmarted often by opposing attorneys. Today, I am freed by many of my thoughts. Part of this process was released when I met a man of great respect for women—I forgot what it was like to have a gentleman not only met me in the airport but actually park, walk in, and surprise me! Chivalry is not dead nor is the joining of two minds through Christ. A great suffering that may linger is the lies that we tell ourselves in our head. We may be desensitized by irrational thoughts that are not true. Stay in the presence of believers who can really see you.

Circling back my trauma was the divorce and the long years of the custody battle. I remembered my husband's infinite words just before the divorce began, "You will have nothing and live in a cardboard box, eventually lose your state license to practice therapy, and then our son." This statement was such a threat that I felt defeated. I lived in panic, and it took five years to improve finally. Fear affected my finances, career, and relationship with my only son. God is my witness to these words; they still ring in my mind.

Before, during, and after the divorce, my former husband tried to take the most essential things from me. These things are my love and attachment to my son, my self-confidence in performing my job, and my self-love. Some of the interpersonal damage cannot be rectified or repaired because being a mother brings a desire to have your children safe and close. I could no longer take my son to the doctor when he called from school if it was not my "parental day." I could no longer drive my child to school and hear about his daily events. I could not make his favorite meals or cookies when I wanted to, but only on our pre-arranged court days. I was being stripped of many motherly things that were being taken advantage of.

However, there are three things he could not take from me: my sweet memories, soul, and steadfast faith—these are where they need to be. Yours can be, too; remain grounded and know who you are. Be strong and know nothing can last forever, and there is a place of rest that will come one day with your maker. Our earthly troubles will all be far from us, and never another tear. God has you through it all. He is refining you to be better in this life. You will make it through!

Healing is knowing just how to pace yourself. We are all uniquely different and will heal in our own time. We do; however, all must be willing to share our stories, ask for help, receive support, and look the lion of divorce in the face without fear. They may have devoured part of our lives as we once knew, but you will never have to feel silenced or ashamed again. God gave me strength, encouragement, and a voice again after twenty-one years of an awful experience. Harsh challenges you will come to know as you heal. Commitment will have a new meaning, and honoring God will be more intense. He is your Father and wants good things for you. There is always hope for reunification through faith and time.

Psalm 23:5 states that I will be seated at the table of my enemies. God will never allow my former husband to hurt me again, and I believe vengeance is the Lord's. Another verse gives me some hope of the pain never coming my way ever again.

> Psalm 110:1 says, "The LORD says to my Lord, "Sit at my right hand until I make your enemies a footstool for your feet." The LORD will extend your mighty scepter from Zion; you will rule amongst your enemies."

I am not looking for power or revenge. I want to believe that we do not endure suffering for nothing. In the kingdom, there will be validation. There were days when I thought of life as a labyrinth. I would wander around, trying to find my purpose in a loveless maze.

I felt like when I was no longer an asset in my marriage, I was only collateral damage. My former husband always seemed to want to be the center of attention, no matter the cost. I know this well year after year. It became so disheartening. But God sees all things, and I am so joyful that I will not live with dishonoring the Lord from breaking my vows.

There is nothing easy about healing. Forgiveness is such a crucial part. I wrote multiple pages asking for forgiveness in therapy. My former husband chose not to read it, but a copy went to our marriage therapist. There was some sense of accomplishment for understanding my part. The following day, I found the ashes of the letter beside my car door. Forgiveness can be a one-sided action. Regardless, I wish I had received a letter and hope it will be delivered one day. Thankfully God heals us in so many ways. Remember all the battles I had to fight, moving into another home so quickly, taking over by paying all my bills, and knowing how to make enough money to pay them, not to mention trying to balance work, discipline, and my son?

My former husband made fun of me in front of my son about being unable to swim, among other things that I "could not do." I am finally learning to swim, and I love it, as it is part of my healing. The refreshing water makes me calm and tranquil. I am painting again as part of my healing and returning to the unique gift God instilled in my heart. Bible studies are happening in my home, which I had dreamed about, and I want to go back into volunteering and am free to do so. There are so many ways of healing our losses. For instance, Eye movement desensitization and reprocessing (EMDR), is a perfect modality for grieving—as well as moving forward—and a completely different approach than talk therapy. This is beneficial for people who don't find talk therapy helpful. Although EMDR may not be ideal for individuals who suffer from seizures, it is a perfect fit for anyone who trusts their therapist, needs to relax their mind during the recovery of divorce, and wants to move forward in a positive direction in their life. Likewise, this psychotherapy technique is ideal for people recovering from PTSD.

With that being said, I have various things I want to do with the rest of my life now that I am free from the constant shame of marriage and divorce. There is no reason that God will not rescue your heart and help you to find peace and joy again. I love and still live by this quote by William Gladstone, which was said earlier in the book, "Be happy with what you have and who you are, be generous with both, and you won't have to hunt for happiness." Dealing with selfish, controlling, manipulative, and authoritarian personalities is complex. Here is how you handle them best:

Toolbox 11:

- Stay calm, and do not play into your opponent's game.
- Set limits and good boundaries so the bullying does not have to continue all day and break your self-esteem.
- Help your children recognize what a narcissist is and how to protect themselves from these parents and people.
- Steer clear of any narcissist traps that could spin you into losing your children. They enjoy spinning you out of control where you feel helpless.
- Avoid senseless arguments that steal your energy or joy, both mentally and physically.
- Ask forgiveness for your part. God sees it all. You are forgiven.
- Pray to God for a path to live the purposeful life He intended for you. Ask him to reveal the truth.

Chapter Twelve

Educating Our Legal Team and What Effects It Will Have on Us?

Divorce attorneys are unique. They practice family law, which is inclusive of wearing many different hats. You will have to navigate many deep waters to gain your sanity. It is an emotional and stressful slew of making decisions that no one thought they would have to.

To prepare correctly, you must have a long list of questions to help you during this process. I want you to understand several things before meeting your attorney. First, you will need good referrals. Begin networking and asking around and know you must work efficiently. Next, begin your interview process. An excellent attorney will need an effective manner of communicating. Not just with the courts but with you! Remember, you do not need to always like your attorney, just like a good surgeon. They pass if they are great at their job and can save your life with proper communication. You will need to ask about their preferred method of communication and how available they are. A lawyer may not fit your standard if you get transferred to voicemail or a paralegal when you contact their office. Ask how many hours they commit to respond to you. Some attorneys will respond to your needs daily or midweek unless in court with other cases, which brings me to another significant concern. Please understand how many cases they are working on and whether they will take on future issues while assisting you. I am sure you have heard that some attorneys start tremendously and begin to dwindle near the end; this can result from their caseload. Ultimately, your attorney needs good balance while being an effective negotiator for you. Understand when your attorney is losing steam. You will need to understand the four parts of getting a divorce in Georgia.

1. Georgia is an equitable distribution state. Martial property should be divided relatively upon divorce. This practice is beneficial if you own several properties. Other things like jewelry and furniture go back and forth until one person can live with the compromise, which is not always considered fair.
2. It is crucial who files first because the person who gets the documents at the earliest is called the plaintiff, and the other is called the defendant— there is much information on who has the better upper hand. The plaintiff gets to go first in court for the judge to hear. I was the defendant, for better or worse.
3. Alimony is not a guaranteed part of divorce. There are a few hoops to jump through and qualify. Proven adultery and abandonment can nullify this right—good look proving adultery in today's declining ethical standard defining infidelity.

Typically, after one year of marriage, spouse monetary assistance begins.
4. Child custody is another tenet of divorce in any state. As a mother, you need a good stomach for this one. Things go so far under the radar that depending on how much money you can spend on an attorney, your children can be ripped from you for years. They will be adults one day, and you may have a second chance to teach and share everything you could never do due to divorce. 50/50 splitting your children is complex and, for many children, is not a good decision.

After you have thought through all of this, you still need energy not to be pressured to settle your case quickly without good discernment and balance it so it does not drag out for years.

Reviewing the attorney's communication skills and availability is good to know if they know the opposing attorney. Though this divorce process may vary from state to state, this knowledge can still be applied anywhere to give you peace of mind and lower unexpected, upsetting issues. If the opposing attorney has a big name with a large law firm, make sure there is no intimidation with the attorney that you have chosen. This information can help avoid conflict that you can avoid. Remember, no surprises! Next, ask your attorney how well they know the local courts and presiding judges. If your attorney is new to the state, ensure they are current with all state laws. Although this may be hard to discern, you can research, too, since you are now a team player.

Similarly, it would help to ensure your attorney has sound judgment. If you are a Christian, they must ensure your values align. Please become familiar with their beliefs about whether you should seek a collaborative divorce, settle out of court, and have joint custody versus sole custody. Lacking this was my biggest downfall in my court case, and I paid for it emotionally for many years.

Throughout this process, whether short or dragging out, having an attorney is vital. They will also need to be emotionally stalwart. You will need support. If your divorce case is as grueling and devastating as mine, you will need an attorney who is both caring about your emotions and savvy with their emotions while doing business with your opponent. They must be reasonable under pressure, whether from you or opposing counsel. Your attorney can never lose control of the case. Your attorney will need to be emotionally intelligent as well as book smart. They must be excellent at finances if they have a stellar accounting background that can save you money. Every time your attorney asks for specific documents, charge card statements, bank statements, phone records, etc., they must be organized and cataloged. These are all qualities worth praying for when asking God for an attorney with a miracle personality who can balance all these demands.

Due to opposing counsel sending mandatory information to us in a disorderly fashion, hours and days were wasted in my case. It was time-consuming and costly to reorganize all the data that they requested. I had to hire a forensic accountant to sort things out eventually. I felt it was a smokescreen to prevent any leverage for our team and drained me financially and emotionally—can you see that was their plan? This divorce game is so taxing on a person that you never know your opponent's honesty and merit until the fight begins.

Lastly, you may spend many months with your chosen attorney. It is helpful if you know all the things it takes to be a reasonable attorney. It would be best if you were comfortable with their bedside manner and ability to rule with authority in your case in the best direction for your future. I prayed for my attorney for many days.

Two more essential items need to be at the forefront of your mind. Who is training our attorneys today? Do attorneys and judges still have unpolluted consciences (after years of practicing family law) in front or behind the bench? Other thought-provoking questions spin in my mind from time to time. Does our legal system care about keeping society wholesome? Are morality, honor, and loyalty even virtues in those training for our future defense teams? Is law school itself supposed to train all these details? I am unsure of all the answers, but I know the following information is growing and grueling.

The amount of emotional, distressing divorce lawsuits is astounding in our current legal system. The strain of COVID-19 is believed to have increased divorce in our nation. Between the virus and the frustrating lockdown from the pandemic, it seems it created the perfect storm. An editorial from writer Carly Kinch suggests an increase of 122% in those seeking divorce from 2020 to 2021[xii].

I believe some divorce cases are so horrific for what a wife or mother must endure for days, weeks, months, and sometimes years. Why is this allowed to go on so long? Why is money so important that you need a lot of it to get a fair shake of a jury trial? How far do we need to go in debt to get a fair shake? There appears to be such an apparent division of the rich and the less fortunate in court and referring that is no secret. It seems such a negligent way of caring for our society in our legal system. I think there is a definite correlation between increased mental health issues and poorly handled divorce cases due to this very issue.

I am greatly concerned not only for my generation of women in their fifties and sixties (Which seems to be when the divorce rate peaks) but also for our children's generation. If statistics continue to grow, then divorce has the potential to continue increasing in the upcoming years. It seems we have forgotten the value of marriage and lost the realization of the human pain that divorces evoke. As Christians, can we do something to stop this cycle? Society is not as willing to always support failing marriages. It seems that many divorcees feel that they were missing out on life, wanted to be more stimulated, happier, or did not have the willpower to put into fixing a marriage. Hence, divorce seemed the easier option.

Let us now transition into what happens after divorce. Have you wondered how our legal system helps us to become mentally stable and healthy again? I do not believe there is a consistent or strong answer to this question. Is this not shocking to you? Why do we accept this devastating truth that our legal system doesn't help us?

Attorneys take many continuing required educational classes on our ever-changing justice system. They enroll in continuing education classes annually to keep their licenses current. The problem is that so few and limited educators are helping attorneys learn more about the various severe mental health diagnoses. While I understand that attorneys are not therapists or psychiatrists, I do believe that these concerns are all intertwined in today's world. We should have mandatory classes in advanced psychology to train attorneys on the details of the emotional effects of divorce and to help them better recognize personality disorders and the help that the partner will need to escape that type of mental abuse, as well as guidance for how to cope with a divorce or traumatic events for their clients. Now, we come to the biggest concerns for our future of divorce. Knowing and understanding who we are fighting during the divorce.

Dealing with Narcissists in Court Cases

There are many types of unseen mental abuse in relationships, including divorces. Unsurprisingly, one of the most significant examples of this is living in secret and dealing with narcissists and alienators. I believe that some attorneys have begun to understand this abusive role that some partners play that is narcissistic. Still, I wonder how many attorneys can fight back with fire to extinguish the narcissist.

When divorce unleashes this war, so much proof must be present; otherwise, winning a court case against a narcissist is impossible. They fight dirty and manipulate the entire attorney team and legal system. Divorce is a well-liked game for a narcissist. After studying various clients and many credential courses I took on narcissism, I want you to know that they generally are above average in intelligence, very clever game players, and well put together on the outside. They enjoy attention and are likable members of the community. The narcissist can be the client or the attorney. Please do not laugh, but most narcissists choose attorneys who mimic themselves, meaning they are narcissists, too. The underdog has little chance of a fair fight against this narcissistic team because the underdog's voice must overpower those more powerful than themselves. Well-informed attorneys are changing our world one step at a time in a positive direction for the underdog, who has been beaten down so badly and has little to no voice. It becomes exhaustingly clear that having a positive outcome with such devious interactions with the narcissist and their followers will be hard.

I always look for just one little sparkle of hope when I hear from my clients or friends going through a tough divorce. The good news, in Atlanta, is that several therapists are putting together workshops for attorneys and judges to teach them more about the diagnosis and behaviors of narcissists and sociopaths. It is becoming increasingly more common in high-profile, high-conflict divorces to have qualities of a narcissistic spouse in divorce proceedings, even if never diagnosed. Let's be honest for a moment: In all my years as a clinician, I have rarely heard of anyone wanting therapy help after being diagnosed as a narcissist. Therapy is a rare request because these individuals do not regularly seek other people's advice. Maybe they have too much fun in divorce court, getting attention and sympathy. They do not see anything wrong with their behavior. The ashes of marriages, through narcissistic eyes, are seen as Exius Actos Probat, which is commonly mistaken as the ends justify the means. Still, the results signify the means justify the ends.

According to Lawyer.Edu.org, in 2022, the main classes a lawyer takes in school include:

- Legal writing
- Transactional drafting
- Advocacy skills
- Criminal law & procedure
- Civil law & procedure
- Contracts
- Real property
- Torts
- Wills/trusts/estates

Electives, such as:

- Immigration law
- Intellectual property law
- Environmental law
- International law
- Domestic relations
- Juvenile law
- Consumer law

While every one of these classes is essential, where are the classes focusing on restoring their quality of life, understanding mental health and statistics about women committing suicide, and the long-term physical and mental health issues that happen from divorce? Should we not require more psychology courses for these fresh, aspiring attorneys from law school? All legal, accounting, and counseling professionals must go through continuing education for credentials. Although nothing is mandated yet, it would be beneficial for these lawyers to take classes to improve the mental health of those less fortunate during and after a divorce. Would it not be wonderful if our divorce attorneys, whom we trust with our lives and finances, better understood the severe effects on women and children during a separation? A year of paid therapy would be a good start for anyone losing their marriage and family.

One of the main issues of divorce is that many of us cannot sustain our marital commitment once our spouses meet strong and successful attorneys who show them the power they can leverage in divorce. The divorcing spouse generally wants their attorney to help them learn all the loopholes and be better informed about giving less and coming out on top in a divorce, especially if they cheated or want the divorce for the wrong pretenses. (This strategy is a significant gain because they become privy to the caveats of divorce by being the first informed about details.) It seems attorneys can have much power and influence when they assist their clients in deciding to end a marriage, although there are always exceptions. They can make it seem like a business transaction without any emotional attachment, which appears enticing for some spouses. This emotional detachment can be beneficial when someone is physically and emotionally suffering due to abusive behaviors by a partner. In times and situations like these, lawyers are good at helping us protect ourselves from further damages from our spouses.

The horror of fighting against attorneys changed me forever. There will always be some devious people who seem to operate under the radar regardless of their job. I guess there will continue to be people with a nefarious character who do not care or notice who and what they are destroying. I felt my world spin upside down with opposing counsel. I am not the same person anymore after the abusive battle I fought. I was forced to sign non-disclosure agreements and did not want to because it was just another way to silence the truth. After two straight days of mediation and war, it was clear that I had to sign or go to court. Why should anyone not be allowed to talk about their marriage experience candidly? Truth is truth, but it is not always easy to prove when fighting a financial war of divorce. It seems everyone has an agenda. I almost felt at times that I was playing a game of poker, which looked like a waste of my experiences and stories that I would not ever be able to tell. So many mothers and single women could benefit from knowing the truth, so they never have to experience the same thing.

Not all marriages headed for divorce actually end poorly. Divorce lawyers and marriage therapists report that some couples are more motivated to remain married due to their financial positions, social status, the comfort of health insurance, and saving face for their children[xiii]. They, however, live two separate lives. According to federal law, an ex-partner qualifies for a share of a spouse's Social Security payment. This law is tricky because the marriage must last a decade, and the receiving partner cannot remarry. In the case of more amicable divorces, financial advisers and lawyers may urge a couple married under ten years to wait until the dependent spouse qualifies, so it is more of a "win-win" situation for both.

At the time, my choice seemed anything but kind or amicable. There was no "win-win" position in my marriage for me at the time of divorce. If anything, it was to save as many ounces of blood as I could to keep living. I was in my mid-fifties, and understanding the true meaning of a dead marriage was incomprehensible. This idea of a lifeless marriage came from a book that my mother-in-law gave my husband to read, *Divorce, God's Will*. Do I say more? I began to see that no separation would have helped us, and I did not have the luxury of any conversation with my former husband. Instead, he shot down every idea and act of apology that I gave him. He could not fathom the thought that I may be right about circumstances that happened. It seemed that he had long decided that divorce was his best option.

I lived through many experiences being bullied as I saw it. I could do nothing right and had little to no good ideas. For many years, I watched my former husband belittle me into feeling like a maid, babysitter, and a warm body in my home. I was not a saint, but in my defense, there is only so much a human can take lying down without some correction or change. I know I was, and still am, a peacemaker, as I tried hard to salvage the marriage day to day and month after month. Unfortunately, my efforts only led to the sorrow of having someone else tear down my esteem, character, and confidence for things I have little control over in a frail condition as I was. No attorney in the world can put a price of retribution in divorce for all those issues I experienced. My relationship with my parents even differed during the divorce, which is not replaceable in a court of law.

Furthermore, divorce can even change your relationships with some friends and colleagues. I lost my best friend from college, whom I knew longer than my husband. It was a thirty-year friendship; she was at my wedding and was at the birth of my only child while on life support. I loved her like a sister. She was a friend for so many important events in my life. Soon after my divorce, the friendship also ended forever due to a situation in my case. The devastation was immense, leaving me heartbroken to lose my husband and good friend. I may have cried as much or more for her because I knew her longer than my marriage. The divorce and loss were so damaging to me, allowing me to experience fear and evil on a level that I had never thought possible.

My experience leading up to the divorce was brutal. I never felt I could come up for a breath of air and was suffocating in grief. I felt like I was on a time clock to hire an attorney to help reduce the constant assaults and accusations on my character, as my former husband also challenged my cherished values as a mother. The opposing counsel seemed to have a tactical plan to break me into pieces and spin pure chaos. Know this: A well-seasoned attorney will stop the game-playing and reveal and expose the person for who they really are. However, this is never easy, especially when dealing with a narcissist. Without your attorney's help and complete understanding of this crusade, over time, this will destroy your self-esteem and self-confidence, let alone any love and decency for the fading marriage at the time of divorce.

My story came down to who would serve the other first. Some attorneys believe this ultimately has some power over the process of divorce. Well, I was done with the papers first. I will never get over being subpoenaed by a server in my driveway on the Friday before Mother's Day. The server waved to me as if she knew me and then threw the letter at me in the car and stated, "You have been served." Afterward, my son and I drove to Nashville that weekend to watch the famous pre-Kentucky Derby event called the Iroquois horse races. I kept my tears inside for most of the drive as thoughts drifted in and out about the divorce papers. The brutality and manner of treating a wife after twenty-one years of marriage devastated me.

After arriving at the hotel, my son told me, in front of two dear friends we met at the hotel, that he did not have money even to buy me a card or small gift because his father told him I did not deserve anything. Moreover, he was told by his father, "She is not my mother, so why would I help you buy a gift?" These words took my breath away. How would my son even navigate life with women in his future if he believed such things? Here is a demonstration of the type of bullying I experienced in my marriage and after the divorce, which can leave an entire family in despair and cause mental illness to creep in with all the mixed-up emotions into the offended spouse.

Later, as we arrived home after the horse races, the opposing attorneys subpoenaed me to obtain all my diaries. It felt like they wanted to try to exploit my private life in court while beating down my character. I wanted to go to trial and take a chance on my peers hearing my side of this unfolding story. I wanted justice for what I was experiencing, but this never happened. I spent my entire savings, over $100,000, to go to court and was told it most likely would be another $100,000 to go to trial. There was insufficient financial support to step foot in a trial, even though opposing counsel threatened to do so.

Instead, there was mediation for my divorce, which was calculated and doomed from the start. I would never have enough money to go to trial. There was so much that I wish I could have recorded and made a movie for others to see how dumbfounded I was during this legal endeavor. No counsel could explain the mounds of unanswered and undiscovered information in mediation. The clock was always ticking away and costing hundreds of dollars an hour. I wanted everything exposed and all the details to be noticed, but this never happened. I even had a book of pictures from a well-established private investigator regarding my former husband's activities, but the media did not use it.

The truth is that some mediators do not care what goes on in a marriage related to specific topics. A council member confirmed that a judge rarely cares anyway. It is recognized in America that poor choices of bad behavior happen in marriage, and you are to move out or move on. This state of acceptance is rigid for me because I never grew up or was taught about marriage or relationships with this callous belief. Our world is leading individuals in our society with temporary solutions to working out long-term relationships.

Some men are well-groomed and protected to know what to say and how to say things nicely. Not that they are honest communicators but that they know how to manipulate their words to fit any situation. In my case, it was apparent I would never make it to trial because that was a costly endeavor. The twisted life that happened behind closed doors would never go public unless we went to trial. I never understood why we would never even have a chance at trial, except by God's grace, and it was more than likely a great hedge of protection over me to be spared of the stress and humiliation. My beliefs were just the opposite; I continued to have false hopes of going to court after each mediation session.

My married life story would have made an unstoppable and incredible movie. My former husband's bankroll was impressive, making tremendous amounts of money a year. His financial success is why I needed to find a savvy and honest forensic accountant to hire. However, The high-profile person I selected never could keep up with the ever-changing money trail. I wondered what was wrong with him and why he could not focus.

On the second day of mediation, close to the tiring end of the pre-holiday day, I was given a list of jewelry received as gifts. I thought it odd and despicable to be asked to pay for my diamond ring, which I waited until my tenth year to receive, and a few pieces of designer jewelry amounting to approximately several thousand dollars. I needed to pay for them if I wanted to keep them, yet my former husband and counsel had not informed me of this before mediation. He had all the receipts bundled up, and I had only one ticket for the jewelry. I wondered about all the lovely gifts I had given him and never lowered myself to that standard. I had no choice but to run home and find these jewelry pieces so I would not have to pay for them. This outcome was bewildering and upsetting for me. It was such an immature and deliberate stab at an uncontrollable situation for me to escape. I think it was to get me off the track of the various never-ending unsolved and money trails, which all ended in question.

After the divorce, I discovered that many forensic accountants have suspicious and close connections with attorneys. Though I had no evidence, I felt like Alice in Wonderland falling down an endless rabbit hole and wondered if this affected the performance and quality the accountant gave me. This truth is why it is imperative to know who you are in the chess game of divorce while praying that your Heavenly Father protects you from cheating and secret relationships. Discovering their motives after the fact will not help your case, so vet who works for you before hiring your legal team. Know the good old boy network and who greases whose hands.

So, now I would like to unveil the emotional game of divorce as much as possible:

1. Winning is hard if you are the underdog making a modest living; the money goes too quickly.
2. You may be able to negotiate a fee that covers the entire divorce, whether it is quick or takes several months. That is the best scenario. (I wish I had known that strategy earlier in the process.)

3. In some states, it is possible to recover financial damages after divorce, if the wounded spouse has proof of financial records showing a timeline of spending marital money on the mistress.

Unfortunately, it is difficult to prove the emotional abuse from finding this information out for the other spouse. Having several private investigators and forensic accountants on the payroll costs a lot. Even then, many judges do not have the emotional tolerance to listen and rule in your favor. They see a well-dressed spouse come into the courtroom and underestimate her need for financial support due to the spouse's decision to disrupt her life. However, in certain states, you may have a civil suit for the person who has an affair with your spouse for emotional damages with enough proof.

I remember I never saw all the financial bank and charge card statements until the end of the second eight-hour mediation session. My counsel told me I would not have made it through the various mediations due to the hidden, shocking content. Seeing the endless and reckless choices of where our marital money went was disgraceful. The private investigator followed my former husband to a hotel outside of our state. He watched as my husband and a lady went in and out of boutiques and stores, walking out with various packages. The phone itemized records were the hardest to accept. I looked at several years of data on particular dates of my birthdays, Valentine's Days, and Christmas', where he spent time chatting with the same person he traveled with. Having time to call another person on special family days, nights, and weekends seemed odd. It was devastating seeing what I saw in the black-and-white print. At least there was a factual element of the divorce that could not lie and gave me some reprieve of truth that I had suspected for years.

As a therapist, and after speaking with dozens of clients, I have found that the abuser in the relationship typically downplays their behavior to bring more attention to their spouse's behavior. The smartest physical abusers leave no physical injuries that can prove the degree of harm they have done to their spouse. They leave them looking like a failure and worthless.

According to a report in *Psychology Today*, emotional abuse often begins with blaming. Abusive people are often anxious and angry, especially when things do not go their way, or their tempers get the best of them. They insinuate the other person is always at fault. These types of abusers come from a long history of controlling families. Generally, the control fanatics often have experienced abuse themselves and live secretly with feelings of fear, frustration, and isolation. Blaming others and twisting the truth comes as natural behaviors due to their feelings of inadequacy and failure. There are many types of emotional abuse, and I have experienced each of these for many years in my former marriage:

- Yelling or flying into a rage over minor incidents.
- Name-calling and making taunts about your abilities or appearance.
- Putting down your ideas and attempting to diminish your accomplishments.
- Stonewalling and refusing to speak or engage in conversation and activities.
- Flirting and making suggestive comments about others to make you feel bad about yourself.

Psychology Today[xiv] states emotional abuse can be more psychologically damaging than physical abuse. Victims are more likely to blame themselves after many tormented years of being told they overreact or are too sensitive. I remember when he told me to "Stop wearing my heart on my sleeve," three months into the marriage. It felt like he was scorning me. There was no room for crying, and it was unacceptable for me to be able to express my feelings. I still wonder how I stayed for so many years in my marriage.

The other type of abuse seen in some divorces is the physical aspect. It is hard for me to understand why one human being wants to use punishment toward another person in rage, as these people have a giant lack of self-control and empathy. However, the problem is our legal system is not tough enough on these people. They generally hurt or kill several times before being temporarily stopped or sent to prison. I believe the violence gets worse in prison. People with sick minds enter prison, where they can better be around other violent offenders, consequently teaching them more behaviors of destruction and rage.

I know a personal case that I was closely involved in where a client's husband abused her since the beginning of their marriage. The abuse was not only physical but also mental. Her testimony is shocking and true. It will show how severely sick one man's plan destroyed a family. He did everything to prevent her from finishing her schooling. He manipulated their children to believe their mother was a terrible person. He tried to make the courts think she was mentally ill and should not have the children. He moved from state to state and followed her, demanding access to the children. The end of this story demonstrates God's goodness.

How do situations with these results seem like the best solutions our justice system can develop? This case lasted three years, but issues like this are common. Charm and charisma are common traits for these manipulative and abusive individuals, and courts buy into them. They live and operate under the radar, and the public is uneducated about mental illness and abuse spreading in our world. Our courts need more wisdom, training, and discernment when dealing with these humans who can roam the earth and destroy one life after another. It makes me think of senseless killing in America, and the killer gets to live. Why is this? Has justice slowly turned downward to less punishment or correction for these people? How many more people must be victims of this twisted and distorted behavior? Better yet, how many more innocent lives need to be interrupted and inflicted pain before our world demands better justice?

There seems to be a common theme in our courts. Expressing feelings and telling the truth can sometimes be your worst enemies versus lying, twisting the truth, and showing no emotion in court. I must have interviewed eight lawyers for my divorce case, as I wanted to be well informed on the procedures. Some had become so complacent about divorce that I cut my interviews short and left. A few others understood that my truth was not well received, nor would it be what a judge can easily have compassion for. Many of our judges are overworked, may not have the ideal family lives themselves, and do not have the energy to listen to the intricate details of those living with abuse.

I knew I needed a passionate attorney who understood I would display a variety of emotions during my case. I needed to be authentic by expressing the pain and sorrow I was experiencing due to the damage he caused. I did not want to act as though signing divorce papers was like signing a receipt for a cup of coffee. My marriage mattered, my child and all I had gone through to keep his health afloat mattered, and I counted.

I found three firms that I enjoyed working with throughout my divorce proceedings. The first one was a Christian attorney and his sweet female partner. They were probably in their late thirties. They balanced one another marvelously. I got to know them almost like family, as they must have seen hundreds of torrential downpours of tears from my eyes during the process. They explained that I needed to be strong on the outside, even if I was drowning on the inside while in court and during other legal proceedings. I put much effort into being courageous but could not always muster the needed demeanor. I was not a good poker player and could not keep the mask on long enough. Also, it is noteworthy that, in the legal world, some judges have lost their edge or compassion regarding the human need to display valid emotions from the plaintiff, whether anger or sorrow. That is generally viewed as a weakness and slows down the court, as they want just the facts so that the court can run smoothly and move on to the next case.

Another thing to understand about divorce court proceedings is that facts can become distorted, and some truths cannot be obtained in time for court, leaving the party destined for loss. These tactics are why it is critical to meet with your attorney before any disposition and talk through it. No one should ever show up to court while still personally preparing with their attorney.

Sometimes, like in my case, the judge could not find the truth, thanks to unfair timing and finances. I remember sitting in the courtroom and having seven people with me for a custody and financial tax hearing. I never dreamed anything could go sideways because there was so much evidence in my favor in the case. A well-esteemed and professional man who I had known for years got on the stand on my behalf. He was well-known in the community and had an excellent reputation for many years. He also knew and had worked with my former husband. He explained that my former husband never filed the taxes on time for many years, along with many fees and fines, causing us to lose thousands of dollars annually because of failure to manage money appropriately. In this particular year of divorce, the taxes got paid on time and overpaid by somewhere in the range of $100,000. Not only was this odd, but half of this was marital money. My attorney requested a tax refund for half, and then this man was dismissed by the opposing counsel and ruled out as insufficient testimony. The judge allowed my former husband, who made twenty times more than I did, to keep the entire refund and for no further reprisal of wasted money from our marriage to be repaid to me.

Then, the custody complaint began. Once again, I had selected a wonderful Christian counselor for my son. After the therapist told me that my son was not respecting their time and not making progress, he wanted to discharge him, and I allowed it. My son disliked his therapist and getting him there was a battle anyway. I was doing all the work driving to and from the office. It was exhausting to head on the journey there and back home. I found another therapist only five minutes from our home and sent letters to my former husband explaining the situation. He never responded until the court subpoenaed me, another battle I lost. My attorney could not prove that I had adequately notified my former husband, even though thirty days had passed before my son went to the second esteemed counselor. At this point, I felt hopeless and had to accept the unfair court ruling. I paid what was due and had the transcripts to read, overthinking that I had done something wrong. I spent for two new attorneys to read the transcripts. Everyone sided with me but explained it is hard to overturn a ruling and very expensive. I knew my former husband had so much money that I could not fight a fair battle in court or anywhere else.

A person going through a divorce for the first time does not always understand the countless issues they will encounter. Many of these things are financial, devastating, and emotional losses. Understand that meeting with your attorney much more often than expected is common. You will pay more than you think because you cannot predict how your spouse will play their cards. Sometimes, you will become exhausted and feel your world is upside down. It will seem as though it may never end. Instead, consider the divorce an opportunity to reclaim control over your life!

Next, my story continues with the second attorney I hired; one may switch attorneys, should they desire. She was beautiful inside and out, passionate about her clients, and cases. I knew right away we would be a good fit. In your case, it is essential to trust the person advocating for you. That is not to say I found her without a lot of prayer first. While I learned valuable things from my first attorney, the second attorney seemed to have more experience with the powerful, wealthy, and ego-centric husbands. She knew well that the sound principles that we expect to have would be sidetracked and need better navigation than the average case. They often try to have smear campaigns about the spouse, as if they were running for a political office. Be ready for a roller coaster ride that seems never to end. Nevertheless, I would rather the "coaster" than a merry-go-round that never stops going around and around. My attorney knew that no commonly expected rules would always apply here; it is like playing Russian roulette. She was terrific in every way and instilled confidence, wise guidance, and unwavering support in me, which I'm so thankful for.

Here are some ideas and good standards of how to manage a variety of difficult obstacles like ego-centric, powerful, and controlling narcissism from many different court positions:

1. Recognize common narcissistic tendencies. Exaggerated self-importance (feelings of superiority without achievements to support it) is one.
2. Don't engage; they want to spin you and love a good

fight. State this is inappropriate and walk away. Call the police if necessary. Take your phone camera if necessary to document for the court what is happening. Often, the behavior is not believable, so be ready to defend yourself.
3. Shield your kids from the conflict because your former husband wants to drag them in and be daddy of the year.
4. Don't expect mediation always to work. The court systems are so behind that many states commonly require mediation for two rounds before setting up to go to court.
5. Document everything because they can be a mile ahead of you. Everything you remember is just hearsay with authentic documentation. Have a notebook filled with phone records, pictures, their schedule at work and how many hours they are with you or your child, how much they make and you make, home and personal bills, if you pay them on time, their spending habits, people who will testify or at least do an affidavit for your character.
6. Be prepared to explain narcissism to the judge because many have probably heard the phrase but still do not understand or believe it exists.
7. Understand that narcissists are famous for child custody cases, claiming they never get to see their children. Truth be known, if they were not worried about being the social butterfly at every event in life and were not workaholics, they would be able to see their kids.

Toolbox 12:

- A person going through a divorce or separation for the first time does not always anticipate or understand many things they will encounter. The process is long and grueling. Many of these issues are financial and other emotional demoralizing. Find a shield of support.
- You will meet with your attorney a lot more than you expect. You will pay more than you think because you cannot predict how your spouse will play their cards. Think about offering your attorney a lump sum payment instead by the hour.
- You need to understand the four parts of divorce in Georgia.
- You will need counseling and various support groups to keep your sanity during a divorce case.
- Things will be missed or overlooked after court or mediation is over. Move on and consider yourself blessed to escape with your heart closer to God and learn more.
- Money is not the end-all, and you can't put a price on good mental health. God sees everything and holds all justice in the higher places with authentic, divine truth.
- Always take the high road; your spouse may not. They may be unscrupulous and try to hide money or destroy your relationship with your child. It is so tempting not to be honest and live above reproach. Know your God is your Father, and He ultimately wins the battle for you in His timing.

- Think about the divorce as a temporary setback and an opportunity to reclaim control over your life!
- Update your will and any other legal document you may jointly have to reflect the divorce and proper ownership.
- Understand that your credit score will most likely take a decrease. It is normal in divorce. This is only a temporary setback.

Chapter Thirteen

The Aftermath of Divorce

The aftermath of leaving your soulmate, the one you dreamed about getting old with and being buried beside, is neither pretty nor for the faint of heart. But storms, tornados, hurricanes, or other natural disasters are not easy to recover from, yet people do it daily. It is essential to remind yourself that you can and will get through this challenging experience and even move forward with a renewed belief of the healthier you. People rebuild daily and are tough and better for it. In general, rebuilding anything is a lengthy process. If you think about bridges, they take years to engineer, be approved, and then constructed. The engineers must know the bridge's weaknesses and the surrounding area's support. While we are more complicated than bridges, we should still expect to be patient with ourselves and pace. One of my favorite quotes is, "Knowledge becomes wisdom only after it has been put to practical use."[xv]

In other words, wisdom is attained only after the experience of our trauma. Sometimes, the storms in relationships give us a better understanding of life and who we are. Wisdom does not come free; it is costly. Intuition is another part of learning and often comes with a price. A high level of intuition may increase your noted, painful memories. Even so, intuition can assist in gaining truth from those memories. Parts of the puzzle will start to fill in the gaps. Secrets are exposed, and you feel a sense of justice as a sign of relief.

Looking back, it remains like a sharp dagger in my chest cavity when I am reminded of those twenty-one years spent with my former husband. The knowledge I have now, after the divorce, legally and personally, is prolific. It made me realize that this discovery validated so many of my suspicions. After the last moments in mediation, my counsel handed me a large manila envelope. The contents were shocking as I thumbed through three years of phone records and various charge card statements connected to my husband's affair.

I remember minutes before receiving the envelope, praying for the seven parts of God's armor to protect me, praying this often during divorce proceedings, and for light and truth to become apparent. I prayed so hard for God to let me see what was in the darkness. I always felt threatened before I had solid proof of his cheating. Even when the truth is sometimes a plain sign on the wall, it is still daunting to never know in which direction the next punch will come. It almost seemed like a lion was waiting to pounce on me once I caught my breath. God revealed as much as I could handle in intermittent experiences, exposing only truth in such a manner that I knew He could have provided this. What that envelope uncovered was unbelievable. There were details of many things I had suspected but never knew another human could do.

The aftermath was far worse than the beginning. It was almost impossible to believe the end was seconds from the ink drying on my signature. All the promises made to me and what should have been pure in marriage were now tarnished. It was on me to figure out how to get up and ride the horse of life again.

The good does not always prosper in this life. However, I believe God will reward them upon entering the gates of heaven. I found these verses in the Bible that helped me understand to keep shining my light and let go of wondering what will happen to others in this world. Psalm 1:20 is considered the "Prayer for deliverance from enemies."

This scripture helped my heart to understand the wicked will not reign over you nor inherit the earth.

There are many other psalms that I prayed for peace in my heart during this time, "For evil men will be cut off, but those who hope in the Lord will inherit the land. A little while, and the wicked will be no more; though you look for them, they will not be found. But the meek will inherit the land and enjoy great peace. But the Lord laughs at the wicked, for he knows their day is coming" (Psalm 37: 9-10).

The aftermaths of our worst storms often prepare us to assist others in distress later in life. I think of it as a calling in life to comfort others. God has now prepared me well. Some of us will hear His calling and answer the cause, while others will not. We can become closer to God through tragedy or far away from Him. He came searching for me like a lost child, and I was just where I needed to be and ears to hear. I love God so much for what He accomplished for me and for sparing me from living even one more second in pain. I entrusted my husband with my life, and it is so difficult to sit and experience betrayal; it stings for a very long time. My advice to you is the moment you feel trespassed upon, be wise and begin to notice things. Is there a familiar or repetitive habit in your spouse?

By keeping my eyes on Christ, I know I am worth so much

more than I was valued in my marriage. This verse from Psalm 37 prepared me for who I am today.

Aftermath: Mental Health

My pastor once explained an exciting thought: Reversing pain is an achievement. "Much of the pain in life is linked to choices you have made in the moment and past." Our choices to hurt others are often regrettable, and the continued behavior is not what you still want. Usually, it is too late, and I think society is often at warp speed. Many of us are diagnosed with attention deficit disorder (ADD) or attention deficit hyperactive disorder (ADHD). We are a culture of instant gratification and do not like to wait. Therefore, we make many decisions quickly and unwisely, and the aftermath is not pretty. If we are all going to be honest, most of us have made one, or more than one, of these instantaneous decisions. These types of decisions are not safe or stable.

Before, during, and after divorce, countless people need medication to help calm or lift them out of bed. In my practice, I see women who are like people with paraplegia mentally, almost like they were in a deadly car crash. They hurt all over, mentally and physically. These instances are where the diagnosis of post-traumatic stress disorder (PTSD) comes into play. The actions of their husbands are so damaging they feel they cannot continue life. For me, this looks like jumping when someone is behind me. I still fear someone breaking in to get back or watching me. I have many triggers that were not there before. I never dreamed I would go from getting married to being so beaten down that I thought I had little to live for. I was always happy-go-lucky, being so silly that I made myself laugh. Divorce ripped my silliness, playfulness, and who I used to be away from me. Finally, I have regained a better sense of my old self after many years.

Aftermath: Affairs

You may not always have the evidence for the court to prove this point. It takes lots of cash flow and hiring detectives. It also takes a soul that can handle knowing the truth. Affairs are not always our fault. Although men and their parents may blame us for the damage, be confident you cannot make anyone do something they do not want to engage in. That is a simple mental health fact.

Affairs can begin for so many reasons. Medical inconsistencies in testosterone levels can produce very high sex drives. Sometimes this leads to nude magazines, porn, prostitutes, and long-term affairs. It is not easy knowing your husband is cheating. Sometimes, I wonder how many women wait for it to end and return to normal.

The prefrontal cortex part of the brain can assist us in making wise decisions or poor ones. The male's brain does not fully develop until age 25. That is why many judgment calls are not as prudent as those of older men. This fact is not to say that only younger men engage in affairs. There is another time around age 45-50 that men can fall into a mid-life crisis. That is when you pray that your spouse has an excellent Christian mentor and is honest with them about addictions.

Dopamine levels are also linked to sex drives with phenylethylamine, another natural chemical compound similar to cocaine or ecstasy, making it hard for men to control themselves under the influence

Aftermath: Knowing You Were Right

There are many signs that your husband is cheating. Please pay attention to manscaping and particular attention to their bodies; Serious dieting and excessively going to the gym; Sudden interest in Facebook or other social media to find old flames that are just friends; A strong attachment to their cell phone. Once, sitting at a roundtable of wise counselors, I heard the truth about past affairs. It seems that the phone has become well-protected. He was even sleeping with the phone and frequently going to the bathroom. My husband showered with his phone.

Then, the extreme defending that wives do not need to know the swift passcode changes on all electronics. The exciting thing about all these facts is if the wife alludes to any slight change in behavior, it becomes an instant fight. I lived through 5 years of nonstop fighting.

Aftermath: Custody Battles

After the divorce comes the aftermath of possible years in custody battles; if your children are your rock as a mother, this story may resonate with you. You carried them and experienced the physically painful birth; you gave up and sacrificed for them. Your husband worked. You cleaned, cooked, and raised the children for the most part and may have also worked outside the home. You were responsible for the childcare coordination of drop-off, pick-up, sick days, doctor visits, dentist visits, school plays, school award days, teacher meetings, and so much more. Somehow, right after the divorce, your former husband's attorney gets ahold of all the doctors and phone numbers, and he now begins to visit them as if long-time relationships exist between them. Yes, they are jockeying to take the children, as men know the children are a woman's pride and joy. Women still move on after a spouse dies, but when a child is uprooted from their mother, that is almost unspeakable. There are no words. I watched as the poison ran through the veins of my family. It was terminal, and there was still no recovery. Thankfully, I feel we are in remission now, which is good. Here is a great verse to help you know God has this for you and will take care of everything.

> I have a message from God in my heart concerning the sinfulness of the wicked. There is no fear of God before their eyes. In their own eyes, they flatter themselves too much to detect or hate their sin. The words of their mouths are wicked and deceitful; they fail to act wisely or do good. Even on their beds, they plot evil; They commit themselves to a sinful course and do not reject what is wrong. Your love, Lord, reaches to the heavens, your faithfulness to the skies. Your righteousness is like the highest mountains, your justice like the great deep. You, Lord, preserve both people and animals. How priceless is your unfailing love, O God! People take refuge in the shadow of your wings. (Psalm 36:1-7)

Behavior economics is a topic of great study. What about realizing our simple gratitude in life? It seems there are few things in life like gratitude that are as important in life itself as you are reminiscing about it. Many marketers bank on this behavior and profit much from this theory. Currently, some decisions are destructive and do not have good outcomes. Infidelity is an excellent example of this. We can obey our commitments to God and one another or follow our urges, temptations, and sins. There is a pain in disciplined behavior. It is not always easy, but it is a better choice than regret because we can manage our feelings and self-control. People can only live behind closed doors until God exposes their secrets; the final justice is generally up to Him. The aftermath has another side that is quite beautiful after the ashes settle and your heart finds restoration through God's excellent nursing of us. When you can do no more, it is time to pack up the grief and sorrow and move forward. Here are things we can do to help make decisions with great intention:

- Rearrange your physical surroundings to encourage safety and a serene setting.
- Temptations, such as eating, gambling, drinking alcohol, and sexting, can all be avoided with righteous and thoughtful choices made in advance. Stay in church, in fellowship groups, and prayer.
- Remove things that you do not want to do. Replace with positivity like more self-love, building self-confidence, forgiving what you cannot change, and using your five senses to enjoy the meaning of life. Just the gift of sight is fantastic and free.
- Have good accountability: put candy on the highest shelf, software on your computer to instill morality, etc.
- Do what you need to protect your marriage, if still married, and remain wholesome to one another.
- Knowing how important your future and choices are either builds up your path for the future or can tear down your hopes and dreams of tomorrow.
- Choose noble things.
- Strengthen your habits instead of your desires.
- Fill your counters with fresh apples and bananas instead of cookies and candies to avoid bad snacking.
- Convenience is a killer of our willpower.
- Increase your physical temperament now to reap better benefits of your future.

- Renew the right relationships. The author Jean Anouilh once stated[xvi], "Man creates real miracles when they use their God-given courage and intelligence."
- Be careful who you surround yourself with.
- Surround yourself with good camaraderie. You will need others who have walked in your shoes.

I still remember my childhood having night terrors. Here is a short description for those who do not know what they are. They are high emotional, stressful thoughts that transform our dreams into terrifying conflicts. They generally happen in ages four to fourteen years old. My son was twelve when I would hear him scream out. Some words were unrecognizable, and others were clear. "STOP." "STOP." He was so young, and as he woke up, he had no idea what he had dreamt about. I often wonder if it wasn't the words of our marital fights. I remember later that he would tell me I was waking him by talking loudly in my sleep like I was afraid. I was in a wet and cold sweat when I was finally awake.

It is evil we cannot see but know its presence upon us. In court, there are skewed words that a judge or attorney would not necessarily understand to indicate spiritual warfare is happening. As I gazed back at my friends who came that day to support me in court, I could feel the coolness of the courtroom against my body and a sickening feeling in me. The twists and turns were to begin unraveling. After court was over, my friends were stunned at how everything happened—we were all Christians and felt discomfort in our hearts. However, it is okay with me that I was not listened to that day because God sees all things. The law can only protect us so far; it cannot be in the moments that precede us. The following Bible verse I would recommend to anyone, as it instills great hope and reminds us that this world is not our world. There is so much sin, and we cannot control it seeping in from all corners.

One of my favorite passages in the Bible comes from Isaiah 61:3: "To bestow on them a crown of beauty instead of ashes, the oil of joy instead of mourning, and a garment of praise instead of a spirit of despair."

Ladies, always set your minds at rest. It does not matter enough in this life and this earthly court what decisions get made for you. Attorneys will battle your case and many more like yours. Some have good outcomes, while some have dreadful effects. What matters is that your prayers are unwavering. I still pray this daily for my circumstances.

Psalms 54 is considered prayer against false accusations, linked with an ordeal, the taking of an oath, or an appeal to the higher court. Divorce's aftermath is like rising from the ashes, like a rebirth. Things will all be good, so wait for that glorious day.

Last, now you are free to begin a new chapter. It is finally over! Learn to date yourself and get healthy again. This change means getting back on the horse and experiencing things that give you happiness and joy; if you do not date yourself and know what you enjoy again, how will anyone else know what pleases you? Men are not mind readers, even though that could be wonderful. You have changed during this process of brokenness. You can and will develop new interests. Indulge in a brand-new world of newness. You can explore beautiful places and exciting new people. Ask God for assistance in getting to this place. It is the next step of positive progress in singleness.

No woman needs to experience *A Hearts Betrayal,* as I did. Spare yourself and grow to be strong and wise. Use honor and character to rebuild. Forgive yourself for your part and move to the next level!

Toolbox 13:
- The aftermath of a divorce and a final nail in the coffin of a beautiful union in God's home is now in wreckage. There are only words of grace, love to come, and patience to heal ourselves. Never lose hope.
- No battle ends that day; the aftermath can last for many years. Think about the day of 9/11. It took years to rebuild New York City and for fear to slowly diminish. The truth is that there will still be people who live in fear and PTSD because of that horrific experience.
- *The Power of the Other* is a terrific book you may want to read to have other positive ideas for better behaviors. Healthy relationships are crucial in life. Surpass your current limits and become more. Surround yourself with the best people you can find. Reduce your pain by keeping the guardrails close. Galatians 5:22-23, "But the fruit of the Spirit is love, joy, peace, patience, kindness, goodness, faithfulness, gentleness, self-control; against such things there is no law."

Chapter Fourteen

What Is Your Part?

We all play a part in the divorce dance, even just for a few minutes. It happens to be a complex and multifaceted answer to this question. I have learned that time changes people, and the environment we choose or choose not to change still changes us. At the core, I believe most of us want to protect ourselves and our children. Divorce changes everything, even if some never grasp that truth. The need to defend the implications of divorce encompasses child and parent alienation. While my book does not cover this topic much, I have consulted and included many excellent references.

A significant part of divorce is the need to be well-tutored in our legal system. It can be harsh and ruthless in many high-profile and high-conflict cases and needs constant amending. Know your part in assisting your chance to get the respect and recognition it deserves. Depending on the state you file in, some are more advantageous to women, and some toward men. Some divorce attorneys specialize in women, and many have a desire and passion to help women of faith. Be a good researcher—network and interview attorneys, so you have a good mouthpiece. There is a growing number of attorneys who also market themselves representing men. Regardless of who you choose, in court, you need to trust your attorney with your future life, like it or not! They are your voice, and their leverage with the judge and opposing attorney team has everything to do with your outcome.

It is obvious today that there is a natural stronghold on many victims of divorce. I have counseled so many women in this situation. I conclude that those with wealthier incomes seem more willing to risk betrayal than I have witnessed in any other social status. The critical factor here is that other things in life can trump "money." True love and devotion are two of them. Some men seek women to marry of lower economic and educational status for easier manipulation and control. These women are immobilized in some ways and bound to the marriage by strict faith beliefs and rigid finances. Then, some men walked with the Lord, were given riches and power later in their lives, and became destructive with God's gifts and blessings. I saw the continued rise of income, decreased time at home, lack of united family meals, family prayer, exciting choices of acquaintances, and a devotion to business team-building on the weekends indicate changes in our marriage. There was no more extended room for me, almost like my family reduced me to a caregiver, and that was all. You must be aware of this and know there are exceptions to the rule. This supernatural phenomenon of becoming useless and undervalued seems to almost sneak up on you. Money has crazy side effects, almost like a poisonous drug, to make people change for the worse.

You must be aware of what is happening in your household and marriage. God is more significant than we think. I wish I did not accept the lukewarm relationship I had in my marriage. False illusions saturated my vision of hope. Instead, my family's routine involved going to church and then a Sunday lunch. We had settled for a lukewarm relationship in our church and community. By midday, the arrogance inside our home was back, and fighting seemed inevitable to finish some imaginary scoreboard. Expect more and be pushed away from this lifestyle, for it is unhealthy. My marriage survived on a paradigm of looking okay on the outside and inside purely suffering. God hates sin, and I believe He will punish those seeking to end a Godly covenant.

I am from an upper-middle-class family. I married into an upper-middle-class family. Once married, I was in a marital tax bracket much higher than I ever knew existed. Everything changes with money, power, and younger women entering your marriage. I saw the changes slowly over the years, and then they started to speed up like a movie in fast-forward motion. I became complacent and tried to ignore many of the red flags that so many saw before me.

For myself, I am not one for thin and mindless conversation. I enjoy rich conversations about life and reaching the potential that our dreams are made of. I believe I play a small part in healing a minute part of our world through a loving heart and pro bono counseling sessions. I prefer to keep time with others that are deep, humble, honest, and can build others up. I love exciting people who enjoy sharing and enriching my life. I love to be silly and laugh with others as much as I am humbled to share difficult times with someone. These are my criteria for friendships and hiring people to work for me. Life goes so quickly, so why waste a minute with someone who does not love or value you?

I came up with a million excuses. I wish others knew my story and could have helped me out of the long, never-ending pit. Many victims of unwanted divorces get caught or stuck in a time capsule of grief and anger. I want to link the past and present for myself and others. My goal is to enhance others through this book, with knowledge and my personal experiences, because I know what it is like to feel unimportant to anyone in your life when no one will help you. So, your part is to realize that you do not need to feel or be imprisoned; the door is always open, so stop with excuses and make your move. Insolence ruins marriage: stay away from people who reek of this behavior.

That said, I knew when I finally decided that divorce was inescapable. My part was to save my sanity and my child's future memories. Damage control had begun. I had to find a good representation with an attorney to protect me from things too complicated to defend myself. I wanted truth to come out, but not like the case of Johnny Depp or Amber Heard. I need to keep my dignity and honor as a Christian. I did not need one of the biggest law firms in Atlanta, as I knew that was not the type of Godly representation, I would be proud of. I had hired a man, and later, in the continued custody battle, I engaged a female. I hired a divorce attorney who was down to earth; this gave me strength and comfort. Knowing that both my attorneys came from a faith-based direction was superb. It was so lovely to feel I was in the presence of others with spirit-led souls and consciences' and knew God. I remember praying before each meeting and asking my attorney to pray with me.

It was so apparent that my husband had shopped extremely hard to find a large law firm outfitted with women attorneys who specialized in crushing other women and mothers. The worst of it was the apparent unequal financial standing. I felt I was like a lamb going to slaughter. As I looked across the room at mediation, what I saw will probably always haunt me. My husband dressed perfectly in a professional suit for the occasion, but he was unrecognizable to me with his smirks and shrewdness during conversations. It reminded me of the time that I met his new accountant for the first time. He challenged me, saying, "Shouldn't you be barefoot and pregnant at home, not at a business meeting with your husband?" Then, the two men laughed together at the table. I felt that all spiritual relevance was gone. I could no longer see the man I married, a God-fearing man; it seemed he had spiritual amnesia in the presence of other men.

Take heed: Someone can look like a lamb, but a fox inside may be waiting to unleash devastation on your future. I have heard too many times from clients that their former husbands make a pact about custody cases with them, and then they turn in the courtroom, and no evidence is there to substantiate the conversations of the past. Keeping records of violations and wrongdoings is where we can fail as women. We are natural caretakers and believers, trusting even in the worst circumstances. Your part is to document and be savvy about your trust level.

After all the truth came out in mediation, and I was walking out of the office that Thanksgiving Eve with my attorney, I remembered seven blazing torches in the book of Revelation. I felt like seven red, flaming arrows had just hit my back, and this divorce ripped all my body parts, one limb after limb. But I stood up and knew I still had a purpose in life. God spoke to me, and the ending of twenty-one years of my life and my family were no more. God gave me a slight push, and then a light voice stated there was still purpose waiting for me. It was to help others suffering from divorce and other psychological abuses. I want to always advocate for good and honorable marriages. I will never condone the business of home wrecking or tearing people apart.

As a therapist, I will do just about anything under the moon to bring reconciliation to couples. I still wonder how those people sleep at night. I guess they have a lack of good conscience. I think it goes back to knowing yourself well and Integrity above all. Maybe we get lost in this world and slowly lose Integrity, trying so hard to fit in. Perhaps reaching the top of our business becomes more enticing and instills more pridefulness. I think all of this plays a part. If people worked half as hard in marital counseling as their jobs, we would not have as many marriages get off track. A pastor named Billy Graham once stated, "Integrity means that if our private lives were suddenly exposed, we'd have no reason to be ashamed or embarrassed. Integrity means our outward life is consistent with our inner convictions."[xvii]

I think this means that when unfaithfulness prevails in your thoughts and you follow through with plans, you are not a person of Integrity. Many people call themselves Christians, and I am not the judge of this, but I often am confused by those who attend church each Sunday and tithe what is so large it sustains the church from month to month. They then twist the Scriptures to fit the worldly view instead of being what they are meant for.

Furthermore, Pastor Jackson concludes, "A person of good stature will bring alignment between what you believe and what you do, and only then are you a person of integrity."[xviii] Truth is the glue that facilitates that. We live in a season when Integrity and truthfulness are diminishing because our culture doesn't attach much value to them anymore. Getting ahead by manipulating the truth is considered good business in many circles, but I call that "bad character." When we have an alliance with someone and promote secret-keeping, when a marriage hangs in the balance, it does not say much about us ethically. It is a tricky spot, and even that should open a person's eyes to why truth should be vital to them.

Even though it is great wisdom to know what Integrity is, it is another thing after being hurt so badly to bring your broken family members that are left back into the fold of truth. I understand the hardship of reinstating good family values and role models while mentoring our children after divorce. Divorce changes everything. It makes instilling values, morals, and good character much more difficult. Being disciplined and close to God is the only way to accomplish such a task. You may begin by distancing yourself from some friends, places, and family members because not everyone or everything deserves your time, energy, and attention. At the beginning of your new life, limit who has your time. Stay in your light and continued prayer.

Know that change may have been quick during divorce, but positive change may take years to see the abundance of restoring healthiness. Divorce affects your very soul until you feel it quiver. We must know our part. This responsibility is to hold our heads up regardless of what others say about the marriage. Understand that although change is strenuous, divorce is quick, and change is achieved in good timing. There are so many facets of change that must happen. It would be best if you paced yourself in making gradual changes within yourself. Please do not fall off course and get into other relationships too quickly or enter the evil world of addictions. These footholds can be easy to stumble into while healing and hurting.

Be vulnerable to yourself. See yourself. Love yourself. Take time to nurture yourself and your children. Being a wife is so unique and honorable. The sanctity of marriage is so incredible when it is kept sacred! Motherhood is another high honor you may have experienced in your wedding. Hold these children tight because things in a divorce can change your life with your children forever, thus bringing alienation. Your duty as a mother is to fight for your children and make wise decisions protecting and sharing them when appropriate and safe. However, there is a point where you may need to let go of them if the divorce and fighting become lethal. Your opponent may fight dirty. They may be relentless and have few scruples. You will feel so dirty after having to interact within your marriage in combative behavior, mediation, and court hearings. The Bible consistently asks followers to honor and love their mothers. Examples of this truth are found in Exodus 20:12, "Honor your father and your mother," and Leviticus 19:3, "Every one of you shall revere his mother and father."

I know the personal pain when your child is pulled away from you and leaves with your former spouse. They are a part of a woman that no one else but a mother will understand. You may feel so helpless as you sit and ponder how your former spouse sees your children more than you. So many tainted things happen behind closed doors in court. There is no understanding of how unnatural this separation is upon a mother. Judges must know how they destroy children's relationships from many glim rulings like these.

I remember having six people in the courtroom with me, and the judge was enamored by my former husband being in the military. The judge did not know all the little details about him having a choice when his naval ship was sold in the military, having a career choice to continue to serve the country, or leaving and getting out early. The following sentence out of the judge's mouth was how he was proud to see an alumnus of Vanderbilt University. I thought judges were supposed to be impartial. Should I say more? The business of the court is tricky and unpredictable.

I received the court transcripts a month later and had another law firm review them. Everyone concurred that there was too much personal interaction, which infected the truth and reason why we were there. The entire turnout was nothing short of a train wreck. How can someone receive a fair trial when sometimes there is manipulation and an opinion that is shortsighted? My part in this was to hold my head high and know that spiritual warfare can be unpredictable and underrated. I knew I was part of God's army, and proper judgment would be given, though not always on this earth and certainly not in our Georgia courtrooms. Pastor Allen Jackson once stated:

> You belong to your father, the devil, and you want to carry out your father's desire. He was a murderer from the beginning, not holding on to the truth, for there is no truth in him. When he lies, he speaks his native language, for he is a liar and the father of lies.

Jesus is telling His listeners that without a relationship with Him, we are not just enslaved people; we are enslaved to one who is a liar and murderer—the very personification of evil and the opposite of Jesus, who is Truth and gives life. Jesus wants us to know that this is life-and-death serious; the battlefield in our hearts and minds is not a playground where we are engaged in an innocent game. Evil, by definition, will take unfair advantage and exploit the most vulnerable places in our lives. It may promise pleasure for the moment, but it does not intend good for us. We don't have enough strength of will or character to overcome evil because it's more powerful than we are. We must choose a godly perspective because evil will own us apart from a relationship with Jesus and the power of the Holy Spirit."

Do not be afraid to step out and become intentional about your decisions. Check it alongside the Bible and several godly people. Ask yourself if your decision aligns with God's Word. Security is not always good; it can be an idol. God will give you peace about the right choices. It would help if you had supernatural, godly strength to govern yourself in this life and steer ahead in a more positive direction when your marriage ends.

Now is where I explain more about the toolbox provided in each chapter. We all need one; if you are like me, maybe two. We have to focus on what makes us calm in difficult times. I recommend that most clients practice calming skills using our natural God-given senses. Clients can buy or find something of interest for all their five senses. Touch is the first one. If you have an old silk scarf, packing bubbles, a rabbit's foot, a smooth rock, or a tangle, set it aside for our project. Next, I focus on sight. What are pleasing reminders of happiness to you? I use old vacation photos, favorite mentor mantras, flowers, plants, and favorite colors in my home. Third, taste is a fun one. You can keep your famous mints, chocolates, or anything you love. We are designing this toolbox—the last two are smell and hearing. Have your favorite music cued up on a playlist. Have a small vile of your favorite essential oils. It is nothing fancy, just little reminders to find your grounding platform.

Remember that divorce is like a novel, not a short story. It has many chapters, and they are complex. Your book does not have to end after divorce. You have many new chapters to write. Always know when to turn the page in life! Do not let the carnage of the divorce devour you. This end is not *the* end. It is the beginning. Figuring out your part includes forgiveness, which may seem impossible! God wants us to be tender-hearted as women to know the depths of mercy.

Proverbs 28:13: "Whoever conceals their sins does not prosper, but the one who confesses and renounces them finds mercy." Proverbs states what is obvious to anyone who has made that mistake and suffered for it: trying to conceal your sin before God does not lead to a good ending. The only way to find mercy is to confess our sin and renounce it repeatedly.

Toolbox 14:

- We all play a part in the dance of divorce.
- Know your part in assisting your legal case to get the respect and recognition it deserves.
- It is obvious today that there is a natural stronghold on many victims of inequality divorces. Sometimes, we cannot do anything but let go of good merit moving forward.
- Everything changes with money, power, and younger women entering your marriage. I saw the changes slowly over the years in my marriage, and then they started to speed up like a movie in fast-forward motion.
- God spoke to me, and the ending of twenty-one years of my life and my family were no more. God gave me a slight push, and then a light voice stated there was still purpose waiting for me.
- Women are natural caretakers and believers, trusting even in the worst circumstances. Trust is hard to earn but easily lost.
- Stay in your light and continue the prayer. Have a prayer partner to get you through. Go to divorce groups for support.
- Please do not fall off course and get into other relationships too quickly or enter the problematic world of many addictions.
- Ask yourself if your decision aligns with God's Word.

- You need supernatural, godly strength to govern yourself in this life and steer ahead in a more positive direction when your marriage ends.
- Remember you always have a choice. Forgive the hard things before you become a person filled with rage. Always know when to turn the page in life! Do not let the carnage of the divorce devour you. The weak and cowardly among us will seek to destroy, so choose to survive or surrender.

Chapter Fifteen

Divorce and Client Testimonies

There are so many stories worthy of being in this book. Deciding which might have the most significant impact on my readers was a tough choice. I believe that God wants enduring marriage and families for many of us. There are also biblical references to the goodness of singleness. He prepares our hearts years in advance for our husbands. Here are a few notable verses close to my heart about trust and wholesomeness in a marriage:

> Let marriage be held in honor among all, and let the marriage bed be undefiled, for God will judge the sexually immoral and adulterous. (Hebrews 13:14)

> Husbands, love your wives, as Christ loved the church and gave himself up for her, that he might sanctify her, having cleansed her by the washing of water with the word, so that he might present the

church to himself in splendor, without spot or wrinkle or any such thing, that she might be holy and without blemish. In the same way, husbands should love their wives as their bodies. He who loves his wife loves himself. No one ever hated his flesh but nourished and cherished it, just as Christ does the church. (Ephesians 5:25-33)

Love in marriages can reach a level of selflessness that is joined between the couple. I think a good attempt at a pure marriage symbolizes the love that Jesus expects of His followers and the church. It is an understanding virtue that couples must continue in a positive and healthy relationship. We get knocked down, and then we must be encouraged to pick one another up and forgive sins that have tempted our trust. I do not mean that if one partner is continuously back and forth in the same sin, to ignore them and move forward. In that, one's spouse must be rectified and heavily prayed for. This change will naturally occur and reflect through no more lying, renewal in the transparency of his character, and a closer bond with our Heavenly Father; I only wish we all valued our marriages like this.

Tracey Mae Testimony

A woman once told me the story from the beginning to the end of her twenty-five years of marriage. She married in her thirties and had dreamed of a Christ-centered man. She had prayed for a husband who could teach her more about Christ and be the spiritual leader of the household. I remember her telling me the day she met her husband; she knew right away he was the one. However, he was unsure about her and rejected her as a marriage partner, keeping her on a dating potential. Later, as time passed, he still did marry her. I'm not sure of the undercurrent of her decision to stay in the unequally balanced relationship. She seemed so obsessed by his apparent love for the Bible and brilliant intelligence. However, she recalls that they had great difficulty from the beginning as they dated. He felt she was good enough to be intimate with but not marry. Does this ever ring true in your relationships?

Later, he did have her meet his family in Texas. The mother-in-law did not approve of her prior faith or the age difference. He came from a traditional Protestant family, and everyone had to weigh in on the marriage decision. This experience made my client, a very confident woman, waver in her Godly image to be accepted by others.

There did come a change of heart after several years. Once they married, her spouse wanted children after he got his career off the ground and was persistent. She also wanted children and had voiced a big heart for adoption before marriage. She also wondered what the rush was. She thought maybe it was like a fairytale to him to have a good job, a wife, and 2 or 3 children. She quickly learned the covert language used with others would prevent her dream of having an adopted child as an addition to the family. Ironically, the race ended with another family adopting children. How remarkable of a twist. All the constant negativity her husband had said about adopted children was suddenly never spoken of and erased like on a wet chalkboard.

After a long road of marriage, she conceived a child; the child was a miracle. She gave up many things, including her career, for her family. She was happy to be a wife and mother, even though it was a tremendously challenging change. She explained to her husband that she had worked since she was thirteen years old and was hopeful to continue at some point. That point never came for her but instead for him.

The presence of fear began to set in. She never seemed to do enough to please her husband. There were few compliments given or grateful gestures. Often, there was blame for not cooking well and cleaning well. She recalls thinking that the hospital rooms were as sterile as her bedroom. This dismay continued for many months until she believed she was a failure. Sometimes, stepping off the roller coaster is the answer, giving you a chance to think about the big picture. Well, it sure worked for her. It looked good to the firm he worked for, as did going to parties and playing a part of a big shot. When she attended parties, no one cared what she did and only wanted to discuss future business or how to increase cash flow. The next few years were lonely with the absence of what she had wished to have so badly. Maybe it is a fairy tale, but who does not think falling in love and marrying the most incredible man is not exciting? As her life unfolded, divorce became a topic of discussion. Her son even heard the word.

She explained that the man she had married so many years ago was just a figment of her imagination. There was never a man of leadership or genuine love for her as promised. The man was not the godly influence and head of the family that she thought. There was a big house, but never children filling it, nor Bible studies to be planned. There were no longer family dinners or prayers before meals. She worked hard to build a home of laughter, love, and family, but it was rejected.

The client recalled a specific Thanksgiving when she thought it would be good fellowship and ministry to offer a meal for the church. He hated this idea and did everything to prevent it. Every holiday, he wanted to see his parents and rarely wanted to expand the family to other options. She reported that he had a lot of money, and instead of volunteering to help encourage others, he wrote a check. The fighting and hostility grew until they hated one another.

She knew when the divorce began getting closing, many things changed. She recalls that he started attending doctor appointments for their child. He started wanting to take the child to school. He began attending some of the hobbies of the child. Eventually, she said he became the hero and Disney Daddy. The child was so starved for his father's affection that he no longer wanted time with his mother. This child's longing makes sense, and many clients have explained this phenomenon often. Later, things were worse. She explained that her husband would make remarks condemning the child's mother in front of the child. He became so horrible that the continuous marks escalated. Later, he accused her of taking the child's medication. After all these years caring for her child, my client thought seriously, who would blame her for this? It may have been a smoke screen to stall the divorce process. Often, spouses do this because it eventually drains the other spouse of money to continue. This divorce story may have taken the top in my years of counseling. She lost most of her dignity and ability to discipline her child. The child would tell her that she was stupid and was not allowed to let her help with homework. How these ideas ended up in this child's mind was so confusing. Baffling! This client later lost him in a custody battle.

The client often reminisced that throughout kindergarten through sixth grade, she was there for every school event and other activities they planned. People would remark, "Are you a single mother?" many times. It seemed mother and child were inseparable. She remembers that she would go by his work or call work, and no one was allowed to say where he was. I think this game-playing can only divide a marriage. Why would a husband be so cruel? The client won very little at the divorce. She, like so many other women, suffered financially, and the husband continued to make his success.

There was one thing so true about his story that stood out. He was brilliant, but not for God's kingdom. She reported that she often prays for his mind and spirit to be redeemed with holiness as one of God's children again so that Jesus can restore redemptive justice.

Lu Lu's Testimony

I just learned the term "pathological parenting." I believe it is probably a better term called "parental alienation." It puts the focus back on who is suffering and even dying from this pathology—the children.

My client's story unfolded when she met her husband at twenty. They had three biological children and adopted four more. The adoption story is memorialized in a book and assists a nonprofit organization in helping families pay for adoptions. The report commences with a beautiful image. The couple was revered in the Christian community and the business community as being an influential and well-respected couple.

The reality is that she was only an extension of him for many decades. She had an undergraduate degree in psychology and was going to get a counseling degree, but that never happened. Her husband made sure to shut that down. His manipulating strategies alienated her pursuit of furthering her education. He demeaned her and all her dreams until they faded and disappeared. Her husband never realized her hopes and joys during their marriage. She knew she could not make any income while married or after their divorce. Instead, he manipulated her into a narcissistic and controlling marriage that lacked love and emotion. She was only worth something when he needed something from her. His work always appeared more significant and successful than anything she could strive to do.

After twenty years, they grew to have such disdain for one another that he had no affection toward her, such an arrogance that he was so much better than her. He was successful in business and decided she was no longer of value. This act is common throughout the many clients I have served. Her husband was always being who he wanted me to be: wearing certain clothes shoes, and attention and recognition from his church. Keeping up with the wealthy "Jones." Living life as a mother and wife in these conditions produced anger in her that she was not someone whom her child or spouse could respect. This matter shook her to the center of her core. It still shakes her, thus therapy. It is as authentically natural as I can put it on paper.

Her former husband was never a popular guy in school, a nerd. He wanted affection and someone to love him. He desired a big family and the control for all his children to applaud him for all his excellent work. No one else seemed to matter as much as him.

He was never overtly abusive to her. She didn't even realize he controlled her because it was so subtle, and the manipulation issues seemed normal. But it was a one-way street. She was to look out for him and his needs; if not, there was a price to pay. Sometimes, it was not depositing money into the joint account for groceries and other family needs; other times, it was last-minute weekend business trips conveniently with no cell service. One year, she was uninvited to a significant company party, and her spouse chose all-night drinking and fun over his wife. He belittled her and rarely heard her voice. She just tried to ignore her marital needs and poured into her kids instead.

They had been together for around twenty years when she asked him what color her eyes were. He said brown. Her eyes are as green as an emerald stone. Her eyes were just like his. His mother's eyes were brown. That is how he pictured her, and couldn't ever "see" her. That might not have been a big deal if he hadn't been so dismissive and taught the kids to dismiss her during the divorce. Not just ignore her but disregard, disobey, and discard her. The amount of physiological damage done to humans to create this kind of discord is surreal. Her Christian family eventually was encouraged to drink heavily, curse her, constantly disrespect her at the dinner table, and do everything except make him look bad in public.

These shenanigans were all because his ego couldn't handle the thought of him being culpable in a divorce. He had to be the "hero" who protected kids from an uncontrollable mother. She wasn't out of control; she was tired of being controlled, manipulated, and smeared to look inadequate or incompetent. He projected these issues onto the adopted kids and projected her traits onto them. It was sad that her husband manipulated their children to turn against her. She cried when explaining how damaged their relationships were; unfortunately, this is still true today. It appears it will remain this way because he enjoys controlling and toying with her. He does it long enough to regain control, then stops so he won't give his ulterior motive away. But the victims—herself and the kids in this instance—are dealing with long-lasting, deep limbic depression, confusion, addiction, you name it. Pathological parenting destroys a family system and kills the people in it.

She believes he waited until all the children learned to drive and moved out so he could continue the abuse in their marriage; nothing could ever disrupt his plans.

Her relentless fear is trying to rebuild relationships with a traumatized brain, traumatized children, and no viable career path at fifty. Christian women who've dealt with this are going through this, and her former husband is still viewed highly in the church and the business community. No one can see the truth except God.

Psychological abuse doesn't stay just mental. Lulu recalls that he did physical abuse as well during separation. He had been telling her to get out and leave the house and the kids. She finally filed for divorce and protection. He had already cut her off from the finances. She could not legally go without the state considering its abandonment. It became more physical as she stayed in this hostile home and environment. She began recording things for the police. He started pushing her down and getting more aggressive. She thought he would stop all his psychological game-playing if she recorded him in the act, but this didn't stop him.

She remembers hiding the videos so her kids would not view their dad that way. He continued to ruin every relationship with them. At that point, he completely separated the kids and her. The harsh reality is seeing the everlasting damage that does not seem to heal or end. It's been six years for her now. He has got many people fooled, except for God, as she tries restoring faith and hope into the relationship of one child at a time.

Mary Sue's Testimony

I saw her beautiful demeanor right away with her beautiful, and graceful hidden smile under so many tears as her belly was round and life inside. When Mary Sue came to me for counseling, her husband had hired several large firms to represent him for various severe legal issues. My client explained that she did not have enough finances to protect herself in court, and the events escalated. She explained that when he beat her, he did it without fear, remorse, or asking for forgiveness. He wanted her to become more submissive to his liking and pleasing of what he deemed suitable. She wanted me to understand the extent of his wicked temper. She described a man far more vicious than I had ever witnessed in anything other than events in my life. I knew it was so difficult for her to explain the horror. I understood her story well and the parallel of a life that seemed like a replaying nightmare, day by day. I gave her genuine support and empowered her to stand up and try to tell her story. I knew others must be experiencing what we were, and I found it imperative to bring these stories to light. She became much wiser as the months passed. She learned to avoid the abuse and get help for a better life.

When I met Mary Sue, she had two small children who I came to know during our sessions. They were both full of joy and love for her. She explained to me one event after another that took place in her home. The most horrific was when she explained he had beaten her while pregnant in front of his parents and their children. Can you imagine? I was so worried for her safety and her life. After weeks of therapy, she eventually gave birth to her third child. I was amazed she never miscarried living with such an abuser. She continued her weekly meetings with me while I learned of many more shocking experiences with her husband.

The sad part of this story is that he became free as a bird after wreaking much of her life. He invited daily havoc on his wife and within the family. He left visible bruises that were shown in court, only to be later dismissed. He got a slap on the hand but was still allowed to see their children more and more. My client eventually won primary physical custody and left the state to pursue a new life and education. This story has a good ending, but I did not encounter many more.

The last thing my client remembers is her divorce was so nasty that she had my brother-in-law accompany her to a therapist that she had been seeing so that she could ask him to hospitalize her, because my client thought she was going crazy. She memorized the phrase the therapist told her, "You are not crazy." Her husband is the most mentally ill patient the doctor had seen in thirty-three years of practice. He told her that her former husband needed to be institutionalized in a hospital for the criminally insane.

The therapist agreed to continue to treat her, even though she initially began seeing him for joint marital counseling. The problem with this is that he couldn't testify against her husband. She knew her husband thought this therapist would be on his side and testify on his behalf. Once he realized otherwise, he began threatening the therapist.

Her husband was Baker Acted (involuntarily committed to a psychiatric hospital). Then, he had another psychiatric patient call her and pretend to be the hospital social worker to ascertain her intentions. Once she disclosed that she was going to file for a restraining order in the morning, my husband outsmarted me by claiming that she was the one who was abusing him. His case manager sent a letter to the court about this fact, and they still denied her a restraining order.

This same judge became the judge for our divorce and never wavered in her belief that Mary Sue's husband was a "poor disabled veteran" who was being abused by me.

In fear for her life, she and her children fled to a domestic violence shelter, where they remained for almost three months. The judge awarded her husband the marital house, a 4,200 square foot waterfront home, as she said she had "voluntarily abandoned" the house.

The sad fact is that they tried to return to live in this home because they had nowhere to go, but her husband had changed all the locks. When she notified the judge, she failed to rule in Mary Sue's favor by declaring the family access back into the home.

The lowest point of Mary Sue's divorce was when she went with her oldest son to college orientation, and the Domestic

Violence shelter mistakenly thought that they left. They loaded their meager belongings into garbage bags and told them there was no room available for her and her youngest son upon our return. These circumstances forced them to sleep on mattresses on the dog kennel floor for three days until a room was available.

In the meantime, her husband was on multiple dating sites and enjoying life. While she and her son had to get clothing from the shelter handouts and food from the food bank to feed her son, he was buying a Corvette.

During this same time, multiple people filed for restraining orders against her husband, and the judges denied them. Their eldest son, now eighteen, filed a restraining order against his dad the same day his dad injured him; the same judge dismissed him. Two friends, who had tried to watch over her children, so they didn't have to stay in the shelter, and were threatened by her husband. When they filed their restraining orders, the judge also denied them.

Her husband began stalking a woman that he began dating while she was at the Domestic Violence shelter. This woman also was denied a restraining order. Another girlfriend that her husband had also filed against him after he hurt her.

Mary Sue alone filed four restraining orders against him and was denied each time. Two girlfriends that she didn't know filed against him. The judge rejected every one of the nine restraining orders filed against him in eight months.

Nor was this man ever charged with any offenses during this time. However, a few months after he moved to another state, he was arrested for domestic violence by another new girlfriend.

The judge awarded my husband every single thing that he asked for. She lost everything and did not get alimony. She did *not* get half of his 401K nor get half of his pension. Even worse, she was given all the possessions from both of the homes that they owned, and he took almost all of these items and put them in multiple storage units. Mary Sue hasn't even filed an appeal for this because she would have to go to the same judge, knowing she would still rule against her.

Four years after the divorce, her husband appeared and tried to force his way into her house. He left when her fiancé showed up but parked at the entrance to their development, where the police found him. Even though she had a "confidential address" through the county, so that address wasn't public record, the police failed to arrest him, as he wasn't on her property then. He claimed that he was there to see his kids.

In another attempt at a restraining order (with the same judge), she denied it and stated that he was just there to see his kids. If his "kids" (now twenty-three and twenty-four) had anything to do with him, he would've known they were both in the military and hadn't lived with her in years.

Mary Sue moved from that house immediately and will be moving out of state (to prevent him from locating her), although it's just a matter of time before you can find anyone on the Internet.

Epilogue

Elizabeth Kubler-Ross is one of my favorite people for many reasons. She devoted her life to helping other process death and decrease feeling of fear. She wrote books and gave so much to society. Here is one of my favorite writings from her:

> The most beautiful people we have known are those who have known defeat, known suffering, known struggle, known loss, and have found their way out of the depths. These persons have an appreciation, a sensitivity, and an understanding of life that fills them with compassion, gentleness, and a deep loving concern. Beautiful people do not just happen[xix].

If your husband or partner has been put under the wicked spell of becoming smitten or lusting after a new person, it may be a futile battle to bring them back into the fold of a loving marriage. There is a fun fact that maybe worth considering. Not only the scars in our minds, on-going trauma, but also there can be physical reminders in our lives. Now people have an opportunity to donate relics of their past to a museum. This museum is called, The Museum of Broken Relationships. It is not in the states but instead in a remote area of Zagreb. This is Croatia's capital. It was a former palace and became popular in 2006. You can donate your objects and wait to see if it becomes accepted. The museum has up to 4,000 pieces all containing the object along with a description of the pain related to it. I think this is a very clever way to lose a powerful dysfunctional connection and shed some of the pain.

Another idea to ease your connection with grief is buying, Flying Paper, it is unique because it allows you to write a message and light it on fire as it soars into the sky. The flame is put out in seconds by the special paper and combination of air before any damage can be done. This can be seen as a healthy action and remembrance as saying goodbye.

No matter what path you take healing is like a reboot or reset button for you. Easing the pain one day at a time. Getting you refocused for what God has in store for you next in life.

No time in life is ever truly wasted if we believe that God is omniscient. This word is the understanding that only God has maximal knowledge of our world and all circumstances in it. There is no wasted time on earth because God can make up for what we call, wasted time. Do not forget that he specializes for redeeming us. He can choose this time of bewildering to grow us closer to him. What a miracle! I think of God sometimes as a backfilling in our life. He can erase the ink blots and tear stains from us. There is only one requirement, believe that he can. Allow God to rebuild you just as he did cities physically and emotionally from desire. We may have experience great injustice along our journey but there is nothing too big for God to restore. You can think of yourself as a butterfly. You need to be willing to open your wings that may be stuck and overcoming the fear to fly again. Knowing in Christ your best days are ahead.

Seeing a therapist can help put your mind to rest. It can open a door connection with an authentic relationship that is caring and trustworthy. Trauma can be defeated one day at a time. One of my favorite articles I highly recommend reading is *Does Trauma Cause Memory Loss,* by PyschCentral[xx].

Afterword

I want you to know that my heart and soul went into this book. There is so much more that I would like to tell, but I am not privy to write at this time. I hope that my personal journey and experiences have helped you take another path and reach a better approach to your final destination.

Pain and suffering can refine us if we can see above clouds and the higher purpose. This is not an easy thing, but rarely are things black and white; there is middle ground and shades of gray. I have found when we are able to wipe the tears away, and the seemingly prominent tear stains on our faces are gone, we become tough as life has it; we prevail.

Never allow another person to change the course of your life for anything but for the better. There will always be a battle of the good and the evil until the time we depart this life as we know it. Guess what? Good wins.

Your perspective can release anguish your mind has born. Your brain is a fabulous tool that can take you places you have never thought before. Challenge is good for you! The infamous people who tried to devour you will get their day before God. No unkind deed is ignored nor unpunished. Rebuke your enemies and pray for them as God commands. Continue to move in a positive direction. There are many others that share your same scars, and they will find you and embrace your story. Spread your power and insight of strength with others.

You must learn to build tolerance against your foes so that you become undetected and are no longer preyed upon. That takes a lot of work in therapy. Good luck to you, my friends! Thank you for being my reader. For those of you who are reading this book, it is intended for Christian women who are divorced, or are in the process of divorcing and looking for better understanding in this situation and wanting to heal. I intended this book for this specific population of society.

Companion New Workbook Coming early 2024. Great for women's Bible Studies.

Notes

Chapter One: Who Are You And Who Do You Want To Be?

1. [i]Sarah Jeanne Browne, "How to Let Go of Fear, Worry and Indecision," Forbes Magazine, accessed June, 24, 2020, https://www.forbes.com/sites/womensmedia/2020/06/24/how-to-let-go-of-fear-worry-and-indecision/?sh-4958fd78344.
2. [ii] "Quotable Quote: Winston S. Churchill," Goodreads, accessed January 17, 2023, https://www.goodreads.com/quotes/721301-fear-is-a-reaction-courage-is-a-decision.
3. [iii]Ashley Branson, Scott Branson. "DSM-5 Assessments," Counseling.Education. Accessed September 18, 2023. https://counseling.education/counseling/assessing/dsm5.html.
4. Pearson Clinical Assessment 12881 Crouch Drive Fairfax, Virginia 22030 M: 703 598 0763 Toll Free: 800 627 7271 x26 2060
5. Ashley Branson, Scott Branson. "DSM-5 Assessments," Counseling.Education. Accessed September 18, 2023. https://counseling.education/counseling/assessing/dsm5.html.
6. Diana E Clarke, Emily A. Kuhl, October 13, 2014. "DSM-5 cross-cutting symptom measures: a step towards the future of psychiatric care?" 10. World Psychiatry (3):314-6. https://doi.org/10.1002/wps.20154.
7. "MyPersonality," accessed September 18, 2023, https://mypersonality.net/.

8. 5 Love Languages for kids, teens, adults: Dr Gary Chapman, "5 Love Languages," accessed August 29, 2023, https://5lovelanguages.com/.
9. "Lusher Color Test," Psycho Tests, accessed August 29, 2023, https://psycho-tests.com/test/lusher-color.

Chapter Two: Who Teaches Us Commitment And What Does It Mean About Me?

1. Relearn how to pray by applying the ACTS method: Adoration, Confession, Thanksgiving, Supplication.
2. Stephen Arterburn, *The 7-Minute Marriage Solution: 7 Things to Start! 7 Things to Stop! 7 Things That Matter Most!*, (Tennesse: Worthy Publishing, 2013).

Chapter Four: How Real Is Narcissism And Gaslighting?

1. Marie Sarantakis, *How to Divorce a Narcissist and Win.* (United States: Adrikos, LLC, 2021).
2. Rachel Watson, *How To Annihilate a Narcissist: In the Family Court.* (United States: Independently Published, 2019).
3. Steven Stosny, "What Drives Emotional Abuse in Relationships," Psychology Today, accessed June 10, 2015, https://www.psychologytoday.com/intl/blog/anger-in-the-age-entitlement/201506/what-drives-emotional-abuse-in-relationships.
4. Wendy T. Behary, *Disarming the Narcissist and Surviving Thriving with the Self-Absorbed.* (United States, New Harbinger Publications, 2021).

Chapter Seven: The Many Pieces Of Our Broken Children

1. [iv] Wayne Parker, "Key Statistics About Kids From Adult Families: What Research Tells Us About the Effect of the Divorce on Children," Very Well Family, accessed September 27, 2023, https://www.verywellfamily.com/children-of-divorce-in-america-statistics-1270390.
2. [v] Amy Morin, "How to Help Your Teen Cope with the Effects of Divorce," VeryWell Family, accessed December 13, 2022, https://www.verywellfamily.com/effects-of-divorce-on-teens-2609530.
3. [vi] Yael Klein, "The Impact of Divorce on Adolescents." Treatment Centers Evolve, accessed January 17, 2023, https://evolvetreatment.com/blog/divorce-impact-adolescents/.
4. Amy J. L. Baker, *Adult Children of Parental Alienation Syndrome: Breaking the Ties That Bind*, (New York: W. W. Norton & Company, 2007).
5. Amy J. L. Baker and Paul R. Fine, *Surviving Parental Alienation* (Maryland: Rowman & Littlefield, 2014).
6. Amy J. L. Baker, *Working With Alienated Children and Families* (United States: Routledge, 2013).
7. Donna Jackson Nakazawa, *Childhood Disrupted: How Your Biography Becomes Your Biology, and How You Can Heal* (New York: Simon & Schuster, 2015).
8. Lynn Steinberg PH D, *You're not Crazy: Overcoming Parent/Child Alienation*, (California: Lynn Steinberg, 2021).
9. Sheri McGregor, *Done Crying- Healing Estranged Children*, (United States: Sowing Creek Press, 2016).

Chapter Eight: Why Do Men Stray?
1. [viii] Mark Travers, "Is Infidelity Contagious?: And the Protective Strategies Committed Couples Should Know, " Psychology Today, accessed September 27, 2023, https://www.psychologytoday.com/us/blog/social-instincts/202209/is-infidelity-contagious
2. "Understanding the Blessing in Counterfeits," Waiting in Heels, accessed September 21, 2023, https://www.waitinginheels.com/blog/Month/Day/Year/understanding-the-blessing-in-counterfeits.

Chapter Ten: Damage Control And Proactive Behavior
1. Divorce Money Matters, 1300 Ridenour Blvd Ste 100 Kenneshaw 30152, accessed 24, September 24, 2024, https://www.divorcemoneymatters.com.
2. [ix] "Florence Nightingale quote: Letter to Hanna Nicholson (May 1846)" Wist, accessed January 17, 2023, https://wist.info/nightingale-florence/48356/.
3. Provides actionable steps for non-conflict divorces, at reasonable pricing: DivorceTownUSA, 1300 Ridenour Blvd Ste 100 Kenneshaw, Georgia 30152, accessed September 24, 2023, www.divorcetownusa.com.
4. [x] "William E. Gladstone Quotes." Brainy Quote, accessed January 17, 2023. https://www.brainyquote.com/quotes/william_e_gladstone_150990.

Chapter Eleven: Is Authentic Healing Possible?

1. Caron Out-Patient Treatment Center, 1200 Ashwood Pkwy Suite 125, Atlanta, GA 30338, accessed September 21, 2023, https://www.caron.org/locations/caron-atlanta.
2. [xi] Courtney Armstrong, *Rethinking Trauma Treatment: Attachment, Memory Reconsolidation, and Resilience*, (Ney York: W.W. Norton & Company, 2019).
3. Roger Behavioral Health, 34700 Valley Rd, Oconomowoc, WI 53066, accessed September 21, 2023, https://rogersbh.org/.
4. [xii] Stewarts Law, "Carly Kinch speaks to BBC Worklife about the spike in divorce rates during 2020," News, Divorce and Family, accessed September 10, 2023, https://www.stewartslaw.com/news/divorce-rates-spike-during_2020-carly-kinch-speaks-to-bbc-worklife/.

Chapter Twelve: Educating Our Legal Team And What Effects It Will Have On Us

1. [xiii] Lindsay Weisner, "5 Reasons People Stay in Unhappy Marriages." Psychology Today, March 23, 2022, https://www.psychologytoday.com/us/blog/the-venn-diagram-life/202203/5-reasons-people-stay-in-unhappy-marriages.
2. [xiv] Lori Lawrenz, "What are the effects of emotional abuse?" MedicalNewsToday, accessed August 16, 2022, https://www.medicalnewstoday.com/articles/327080.

Chapter Thirteen: The Aftermath Of Divorce

1. Caroline McHugh, "Life and the life changing conditions for kids," TEDx Talks, February 15, 2015. https://www.youtube.com/watch?v=veEQQ-N9xWU.
2. Free resources and consists of 8-week classes: Divorce Care; Church Initiative, PO Box 1739 Wake Forest, North Carolina 27588, accessed September 24, 2023, https://www.divorcecare.org/.
3. xv "Knowledge becomes wisdom only as it has been put to practical use," Dictionary Quotes, accessed September 23, 2023, https://www.dictionary-quotes.com/knowledge-becomes-wisdom-only-after-it-has-been-put-to-pratical-use-source-unknown/.
4. National Board of Forensic Evaluators, Inc. accessed September 18, 2023, "National Board of Forensic Evaluators," www.nbfe.net.
5. xvi Jean Anouilh, "Forbes Quotes: Thoughts on the Business of Life," Forbes Quotes, accessed January 17, 2023, https://www.forbes.com/quotes/4825/.
6. Tesser Mediation, LLC. Accessed September 18, 2023. "Family Law Mediator." http://tessermediation.com/.
7. Tracy McMillian, "Marry Yourself," TEDx Talks, February 7, 2014. https://www.youtube.com/watch?v=P3fIZuW9P_M.
8. "What it Feels Like to Live With a Personality-Disordered Individual," Out of the Fog, accessed September 21, https://outofthefog.website/toolbox-1/2015/11/17/complex-post-traumatic-stress-disorder-c-ptsd.

Chapter Fourteen: What Is Your Part?

1. [xvii] "10 Quotes from Billy Graham on Integrity," The Billy Graham Library.org, accessed February 13, 2021, https://billygrahamlibrary.org/blog-10-quotes-from-billy-graham-on-integrity/.
2. [xviii] Allan Jackson, "Lead with Faith [You are Designed to Lead]," YouTube video, 54:26, World Outreach Church, September 24, 2022, https://www.youtube.com/watch?v=e2MQH4zD6AA.

Epilogue

1. [xix] "Quotes by Elizabeth Kubler-Ross," Leticia Rae, accessed July 20, 2022, https://www.leticiarae.com/home/2017/7/20/quotes-by-elizabeth-kbler-ross.
2. [xx] Nicole Washington DO, MPH, PyschCentral. May 23, 2022, https://psychcentral.com/health/does-trauma-cause-memory-loss.

About the Author

Christine Cantilena Barnes became a Christian when she started to understand the depth of brokenness in her life at an early age. She was able to recognize right and wrong from her Catholic teachings and began understanding what it takes to practice and earn positive moral and ethical standing. But also, from a standpoint in the spiritual arena.

She was baptized as a child in the Catholic Church. Later, she made her first communion, and then her confirmation of faith. These were all steps united with her family's faith. She remembers thinking, even after all the commencements, that there was still something missing and wanted to find more depth in her belief system.

The past glimpses of brokenness throughout her childhood and college years drew her closer to God. She knew that had to be more joy, companionship, and truth somewhere. The pinnacle of her faith was tested and reached before her son was born in 2004. He was diagnosed with a deadly condition called congenital diaphragmatic hernia (CDH) in utero, a rare condition in babies that can require a multitude of surgeries and constant care, with little hope of survival. In her thirties, she believed this difficult journey helped her to see not only the fragility of humanity, but also the amazing connection that comes from extreme vulnerability and helplessness to allow God's will to be done. She is a devoted mother of one son and continues the battle for future mothers walking in the difficult paths of trauma, including high-conflict divorces and finding closure after a divorce.

She was previously married for twenty-one years and now resides in Atlanta, Georgia with one son, Romeo, a kitty named

Lucy Lu, and a retired therapy dog, Blazer. Christine has volunteered in her community for nineteen years with various pet therapy projects in nursing homes, hospice, assisted-living homes, and schools. She currently leads Bible studies that assist others in the healing process of trauma and strengthening their faith. She believes her special gifts in life comes from God and direct her path in helping others in need.

Christine has worked as a licensed professional clinical therapist (LPC) and as a certified professional counseling supervisor (CPCS). She has worked in several hospitals since 2014, serving the mental health public. She was a staff member at Peachford Hospital, Ridgeview Institute, and the various locations of Emory Hospitals. Her training focuses on trauma while being certified in this area (CCTP), difficult transitions, anxiety, prolonged grief, and resistant depression.

Her goal is to serve those desiring healing and uncovering core reasons for negative patterns of self-harming behaviors, suicidal ideation, high anxiety, and specializing in persons facing divorce, child alienation, and relationship separation. She is a proud member of The Association of Family Conciliation Courts (AFCC) and helps families with reunification and testifies as an expert witness in family court. She found that her difficult divorce had a silver lining allowing her to assist others and to give them hope that life can be restored with faith.

Christine holds a Bachelor of Fine Arts from Virginia Commonwealth University (VCU) and has a specialized art degree with skilled training in drawing, painting, and design that can be used for therapy. She owned horses and helped one of the first physical therapy groups in Richmond, Virginia, assisting children with walking disabilities through therapy on the horses.

Additionally, she holds a master's degree in clinical mental health counseling from Mercer University and specializes in dialectical behavior therapy (DBT), sand tray, and eye movement desensitization and reprocessing (EMDR). Furthermore, she holds an advanced academic certification from VCU in Criminal Justice Administration while also trained in forensic evaluations for court and parental alienation. Most recently, she has been a guest on the radio show "Divorce Town" and assisted women in crisis.

Christine believes there is a solution to all problems. Everyone in life has a story to be told. We all want to be loved and listened to. She embraces all eight of psychologists Eric Erikson's Life Stages and Abraham Maslow's Prominent Personality Theory. She hopes this book will educate others to form authentic relationships, see their blind spots, get closer to God, and heal from depression, anxiety, and complex post-traumatic stress disorder.

Christine has many new interests in life. She loves country music, line dancing, and forties swing dancing. Dating has become a new importance for her while living her life with more wisdom and determination. Christine desires to become an involved speaker to help others grow in a positive light and spirit.

WALK WITH PURPOSE

www.ingramcontent.com/pod-product-compliance
Lightning Source LLC
Chambersburg PA
CBHW052135070526
44585CB00017B/1829